Handbook For Today's Catholic Teen

Jim Auer

Liguori
ONE LIGUORI DRIVE
LIGUORI MO 63057-9999

Imprimi Potest:
Richard Thibodeau, CSsR
Provincial, Denver Province
The Redemptorists

Imprimatur:
Most Reverend Robert J. Hermann
Auxiliary Bishop, Archdiocese of St. Louis

ISBN 978-0-7648-1173-9
Library of Congress Catalog Number: 2004107335

Compliant with *The Roman Missal,* third edition.

Scripture quotations are from the *New Revised Standard Version
of the Bible,* © 1989 by the Division of Christian Education of the
National Council of the Churches of Christ in the USA. Used by
permission. All rights reserved.

Interior photos:
Getty/Comstock: 8, 72. PhotoDisk: 18, 33, 34, 48, 104. Artville: 39, 47, 63,
73, 75, 109. GoodSalt: 36, 40, 45, 66, 84, 90, 94. Eyewire: 30, 41, 42, 83.
Digital Stock: 55, 110. Gene Plaisted, OSC: 64. Stockbyte: 103.
W.P. Wittman: 110.

Liguori Publications, a nonprofit corporation, is an apostolate of the Redemptorists. To learn more about the Redemptorists, visit Redemptorists.com.

To order, call 800-325-9521
www.liguori.org

table of contents

section two
PRACTICES

section three
PRAYER AND SOME TRADITIONAL PRAYERS

section four
CATHOLIC MORAL ISSUES
(Life in the Real World)

introduction

You're a Catholic teen. That means the rest of us in the Church need you. Except for those who joined the Church as adults, every adult Catholic was a Catholic teen.

But this is not about "keeping young people Catholic" just so our membership is numerous enough that we look good in front of the world. This is about truth and reality. It's about where we find meaning and where we're headed. It's about understanding the spiritual dimension of life—things beyond pizza and sports and dating and finding a career. Nothing is wrong with any of those things. In fact, they can be positively filled with God. But, by themselves, they're not what life is all about.

> It's about ◄ understanding the spiritual dimension of life—things beyond pizza and sports and dating and finding a career.

Being Catholic means…what? If *Catholic* is just a label we get because we were "born Catholic," but it doesn't affect or direct our lives in any particular way, then it's pretty meaningless. We may as well say, "I'm Whatever," instead of, "I'm Catholic."

This book won't try to argue you into "staying Catholic," and it won't try to persuade you to become a religious nut who has decided to get holy at the expense of enjoying life. (That's not

Why are we called Catholic?

Catholic comes from a Greek word, *kaqolikos,* which means *universal.* It was used to describe the Church as early as the first century, although at that time there were no other Christian churches or denominations. Christians were simply followers of the Christ. Everyone who believed in Jesus Christ's teachings was a Christian. It meant that the faith was intended for all people of all time everywhere. The first split in the Christian faith came in the year 1054. Christians in the east (basically the area we call the Middle East today) separated from Christians in the west (basically Europe). In the sixteenth century, splits formed in the Western (Roman Catholic) Church. From these came the many churches which today are called *Protestant* (based on the word *protest*). *Protestant* is a very general word. Baptists, Methodists, Lutherans, Presbyterians, and many others are all Protestants.

a true Catholic Christian lifestyle anyway, by the way.)

What this book *will* do is present the very basics of the Catholic faith. The first of the four sections explains *doctrine,* which is simply an official word for what Catholics believe about God and how we relate to God. The second explains Catholic practices. (Why Catholics sometimes use holy water, for example.) The third talks about prayer and presents some basic Catholic prayers, sometimes with a small explanation or comment. The fourth talks about moral issues, meaning how we behave— what's right and what's wrong and why.

The numbers in parentheses after each chapter title are the page numbers from the *Handbook for Today's Catholic Teen Activity Notebook* that correspond to that chapter. You'll gain insight from this book without using the *Activity Notebook,* but you'll gain even more if you use them together (see page 112 for more information).

We'll try hard not to be boring.

Can religion be boring? Well, can pizza ever get stale? But it doesn't have to be. Millions of Catholic teens find it interesting and sometimes exciting. Maybe you will too, or maybe you already do.

But for that to happen, you have to understand at least something of what it's all about.

And that's what this book is all about.

doctrine
what do we believe?

1 if God exists, then what? *(7)*

You've never seen Bigfoot or the Loch Ness Monster. Chances are you're not sure if they exist or not; some people say yes, others say no. Chances also are, you don't much care one way or the other. You've never been to Mount Everest either, yet you're certain that it does exist. In both cases, your attitude is probably something like, "If Bigfoot comes knocking on my door, or if I somehow get transported to Mount Everest, I'll deal with it then. In the meantime, so what? I have things to do."

For some people, God is like that. They think, "Maybe God exists, maybe not," or, "Sure, I believe there's a God." But their attitude in either case is something like, "It doesn't matter all that much, at least not right now. If I ever feel the need to sort it out, I'll do it then." You might call this putting God on hold. It's especially easy to do this when your life seems like an almost endless stretch of future, although some people are still putting God on hold at sixty and seventy.

But if God matters at all, then God matters all the time, not just when you're really old and finally ready to start thinking about God. If God matters at all, then God matters when you're a little kid, a teen, a young adult, a middle-aged adult, and a senior citizen. If God has created us, given us every good thing we have,

11

and invited us into a relationship, then it doesn't make sense to largely ignore that relationship.

As with every relationship, that means we have to *know* something about the other person. There are two ways of gaining knowledge about anything. One is to try to arrive at answers on our own. The second is to tap into the experience of other people.

If God Did *Not* Exist?

"You don't really appreciate something until you lose it," a common saying goes. Fantasize for a moment that it has been undeniably proven God does not exist. How would life change? How would your life change? Some people immediately cite two things: They wouldn't need to go to church, and they wouldn't have to keep any rules. The first is certainly true (for some folks, that would free up as much as 2-3 hours per year!), but not the second. It's not likely that society, even without God, would suddenly erase everything on the law books. (And would you want that?)

How would your attitude, feelings, and actions change in these situations: You're at the funeral of someone you love...and there is no God—therefore, no afterlife, no heaven. How do you feel? A parent or other loved one is about to undergo serious surgery for a life-threatening condition. Doctors say there's a 50-50 chance of recovery...and there is no God. Whom do you talk to inside your mind and heart? You see a tornado a hundred yards away heading toward you. What do you cry out: "Dear Laws of Physics and Meteorology, please help me?" You're now ninety-one years old. You probably have some time left, but certainly not decades...and there is no God. How do you feel about your future?

2 what can we know about God on our own? *(7)*

Some people say almost nothing, while others say quite a bit. Try it yourself; it's not easy. You'll have to put aside everything you've ever heard about God and pretend you never heard it. Just from looking around you and examining your own experience, what can you reasonably conclude about God?

You may arrive at some version of what people came up with a long time ago. They observed the movement of the sun and the moon, watched the rain fall, saw the vast expanse of the ocean with its thundering waves, and concluded: "That's big—and *we're* not making it happen. There must be somebody bigger and more powerful than us making it happen." That's a logical and intelligent conclusion.

Few people, however, arrived at the idea of *one* God. They assumed that a different bigger-than-us person or god was responsible for or in charge of each phenomenon of nature, and each aspect of life (love, war, etc.). This reasoning produced the gods we read about in mythology. With no other source of information available, this reasoning was not silly.

People also concluded, quite sensibly, that they needed to have a relationship with these powerful gods. They drew on their experience with very powerful (and very imperfect) earthly people. The gods, they figured, must be like that, only a lot more so. Consequently, they often envisioned gods who threw their power around and who needed to be won over, paid off, and bribed with anything from

> You'll have to put aside everything you've ever heard about God and pretend ★ you never heard it.

incense to human sacrifice. They visualized gods who were sometimes in a good mood and sometimes in a dangerously nasty one, and who sometimes fought with one another.

The concept of one God who deeply loves and cares about every human being and who has promised us eternal life and happiness is hard to come up with just from looking at the forces of nature or from studying the often-violent course of human history. If your concept of God is like the above description, it's almost certain that you have been guided toward it by the experience of other people.

> **Accepting what other people have learned does not mean you're a nonthinking, unquestioning mental sponge.**

This doesn't mean you don't have a mind of your own. It simply means that you have accepted much or all of what you have learned from others, thought about it, and made it your own. Accepting what other people have learned does not mean you're a nonthinking, unquestioning mental sponge. We human beings build on the experience and discoveries of others in every arena of life from cooking to football, from mechanics and medicine, to astrophysics and rocket science. It's how life works.

The question now is, how did those who came before us get this knowledge of God that neither they nor we can figure out all on our own? And exactly what does it consist of? That brings up two key words: **doctrine** and **revelation**.

3 what is doctrine? *(8)*

The word *doctrine* literally means *teaching*—things presented as true by a community based on those beliefs. The doctrine taught by the Catholic Church is contained in a book entitled *Catechism of the Catholic Church.* Any particular individual truth (for example, that Jesus was truly God and truly human) is called a **dogma**. Not everything in the *Catechism* is equally central to the Catholic faith. The teaching about the person of Jesus is far more fundamental than the teaching about the acceptability of cremation, for example.

Catholics believe that the Church has been given the mission of handing on what is true about God and how we should respond to God. Here we have to realize that *what* is taught is not the same as the personality and/or actions of people who teach it. This is true in any area. For example, a health teacher may teach the truth about healthy living but still have an irritating personality and even live an unhealthy lifestyle. That doesn't alter the truth.

4 where do we get doctrine? revelation *(8)*

Most of what we believe about God and our relationship with God cannot be figured out on our own. Where did we get it? The only way we could have—from God. *God told us* or *revealed* truth to us. That's what the word *revelation* means in the religious sense. God included a few things that we could have arrived at on our own, such as the fact that God is powerful. But most of it would have been hidden if God had not told us.

Catholics believe that God revealed (and continues to explain) truth to us in two ways: through sacred Scripture—the Bible—and through what we call *sacred Tradition*. We'll examine each of those separately very shortly. For now, it's really important to realize this: each of those involves a *group* or *community.*

The Bible, for example, didn't float down from heaven already printed. Jews recorded their experience of God in what we call the Hebrew Scriptures or the Old Testament over a period of several hundred years. But the Jews had existed as people of God for hundreds of years before any Bible writing. Early Christians wrote the New Testament based on their experience of the risen Jesus. Much of both the Old and New Testaments was *spoken*, handed down by word of mouth, before it was written. The Bible recorded and further explained the faith that was active, at least in beginning ways, in both the Jewish and Christian communities.

The **Bible** didn't float down from heaven already printed.

5 the Bible *(9–10)*

Catholics, along with almost all Christians, believe that God inspired the writing of the Bible. It truly is the personal message of God to us, and therefore one of the sources of revelation. But in the Catholic approach to Scripture, inspiration does not mean that God dictated the exact words to the Bible's human authors, and they simply copied them down. God left them free to use the images and language styles of their times. God also did not upgrade their knowledge of science to twenty-first–century levels. God inspired writings of *faith;* what is guaranteed to be true in the Bible is *the religious truth about salvation*—not science or even history the way we write and understand history today.

So when the creation story of Genesis describes the earth as flat, is that true in the sense of factual? Of course not. Did creation take six days as we know them? Not likely. It's the religious truth that matters and is guaranteed—namely, that God created the universe—and us—from nothing because God wanted to share life and joy. God left the human authors free to communicate that and every other religious message *in a way that made sense to the people of the time.* This means that sometimes—not for every single verse, but sometimes—we need to learn a little about how those people wrote, thought, and lived.

The Bible is a collection of seventy-three "books," although most of them are not what we consider "book length" today. Opening the Bible is like walking into a library. You're surrounded by *many kinds of writing.* A library contains books of history, fiction, essays, poetry, biography, fantasy, letters, collections of advice, and wise sayings. You don't expect them to be alike, and you don't approach them the same way. For example, even though there really is a Mississippi River and a place called Missouri, you don't expect the *Adventures of Tom Sawyer* to be the same kind of writing as *A History of World War II.* But you know that you can learn something about life from Tom, Huck, and Jim, even though their adventures didn't actually happen in factual history.

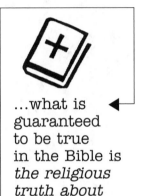

...what is guaranteed to be true in the Bible is *the religious truth about salvation...*

Like a library, the Bible is a collection of many kinds of writing. Some kinds we still have today, such as poetic prayers like the Psalms, and others we don't, like the kind of writing in the Book of Revelation. Many questions about the Bible can be cleared up if we know what kind of writing we're dealing with when we read a certain book. Many editions of the Bible offer an introduction to each book; reading the introduction is often helpful.

Favorite
and Famous
Bible
Verses

"The LORD is my shepherd, I shall not want."
(Psalm 23:1)
This is probably the most famous verse from the Old Testament, and the introduction to the most familiar psalm.

. . . .

"For God so loved the world that he gave his only Son, so that everyone who believes in him may not perish but may have eternal life."
(John 3:16a)
This is probably the most famous verse from the New Testament. It has been said that it sums up the entire Bible. You often see "JN 3:16" on banners at sporting events and signs along a highway.

. . . .

"I am the way, and the truth, and the life."
(John 14:6)
Jesus said this in answer to Thomas' question that the apostles did not know the way to the place where Jesus was going.

. . . .

"In everything do to others as you would have them do to you; for this is the law and the prophets."
(Matthew 7:12)
The first part of this verse is often called *The Golden Rule*— but many people do not realize that Jesus spoke it!

All of this does not mean most of the Bible is too mysterious for average people to understand. For example, when Colossians 3:9 says, "Don't lie to one another," you don't need a university full of Bible scholars to help you figure out what that means.

6 Tradition *(10)*

Unlike many Christians (with whom we should not argue unpleasantly on this), Catholics do not believe that every kernel of God's message is necessarily contained in Scripture word for word. Jesus promised the Holy Spirit to guide us as a community in understanding God's message. So, we believe that the experience of the Church and official Church teaching is likewise a source of revelation. A good example is the documents that came from the most recent Church council, which we usually call Vatican II. Like all of Tradition, they do not *change* anything in revelation and they don't *add* something brand new to it. They expand on and apply God's message to modern times.

It's somewhat like this. Let's say that an ancestor of yours set down some true principles and wise advice for the family to follow. Years later, and perhaps in very different circumstances than those in which that person lived, your family gets together, thinks anew about what he or she said, and talks about it. As a result, they understand better than ever what it means and how it applies to their particular situations. Tradition works like that, except that we're dealing with much more than some wise advice. We're dealing with God's revealed truth.

7 faith (and questions and doubt) *(10–11)*

Even though faith seems to deal with the question, "What do you believe?" there's a step before the "what." That step is "who," and the "who" is God. Faith is not just saying, "Yeah, okay" when you read, hear, or recite the Profession of Faith at Mass. Faith is a response to an invitation from God.

Let's use an example from a very different level. Someone asks you to go out with him or her, or even to marry him or her. When you say yes, you're responding to *a person who wants a relationship with you.* Do you know everything about the person? Of course not. Do you understand everything he or she does, and can you prove everything he or she says? Not likely. In spite of that, you say, "Yes. I will *be with* you." Why? Because of who he or she is.

Your response to God and God's invitation is like that. You're not responding to a list of statements or even to one or more human beings. You're responding to God. Along the way, other human beings usually play an introductory role through what they say or write or through the example they give. In fact, that's the way God usually works. Faith itself is embracing a relationship with God.

A word about faith and mathematics: they're not the same. They're not even similar. You can take two pencils from your left hand and two from your right hand, put the pencils together in a pile, count the total, and *prove* that 2+2=4. If you previously had doubts, you can look at the total and say, "Two plus two really *is* four! *Now* I get it!"

The Man Who Sort of Believed

If you wonder how strong (or how weak) your faith is—or if you *know* your faith is there, but not as strong as it should be—you have company. The Gospel of Mark, 9:14-29, recounts a totally honest response from a man who asked Jesus to cure his son—*"if you are able to do anything."* Jesus pointedly reminded him of the need for faith. Verse 24 records the man's gut-honest prayer: "I believe; help my unbelief." That was a brief way of saying, "I do believe...well, kind of...not as much as I should, I know, but...it's better than nothing, and I *want* to believe more strongly, but I need your help to do that." It's okay to pray a prayer like that if that's where we are on faith. God prefers honesty over "correct" flowery words that don't say what's in our hearts.

Sometimes we want to do that with matters of faith. It doesn't work. If we could prove everything we believe about God and our relationship with God, we wouldn't need faith. We wouldn't even use the word. We'd call it "religious logic," or some phrase like that.

Faith is not just saying, "Yeah, okay" when you read, hear, or recite the Profession of Faith at Mass.

So, faith is just that—faith. Not math or science. What about someone who doesn't believe, or who finds it hard to believe certain things? Faith can be difficult, and a person may have doubts for many reasons. One of the reasons, of course, is that the person may *want* to have huge doubts and may even help them grow. Life seems easier that way, and he or she is free of the consequences of faith—such as living it!

But there are many legitimate and understandable reasons for doubts and difficulties with faith. They are not the sign of a bad or weak person. Mature faith is not kindergarten stuff. The solution is to face doubts and difficulties honestly for as long as it takes, sincerely *want* to resolve them one way or another, and ask for help, including from God, in dealing with them. God is not going to respond, "You have a *problem* with this? That means *you've* got a *problem!*"

8 God: a Trinity *(11)*

One God. Three Persons. Not three gods. Not just three aspects or ways of looking at the one God. **Three distinct persons**—in *one* God. The Trinity is a doctrine that could have come only from revelation and can be dealt with only by faith. Thinking about the Trinity does not prompt people to say, "Well, when you come down to it, it's pretty logical, kind of common sense." Without revelation, the idea would never have crossed our minds.

The New Testament contains many references to the Father, the Son (also called the Word), and the Spirit as having qualities that can belong only to God. At the same time, Father, Son, and Spirit are also described as distinct, separate persons. The conclusion is three Persons in one God, a Trinity. It's a huge, central doctrine of the Catholic faith that will never fit into our minds. We will never someday say, "Oh…now I see how that works!"

But an image might help. Picture three people standing in a circle with their arms around each other. They begin to whirl around and around—so fast that they become one whirling blur. Yet, within that one whirling blur there are three separate persons united by the whirling motion. Father, Son, and Spirit are united not by an extremely rapid whirling motion, but by intense love.

9 the Father *(11–12)*

In our Creed, God the Father is described as Creator of heaven and earth. Although the Trinity is one God, that doesn't mean that the Father alone created the universe while the Son and the Spirit just watched and admired, waiting for their turn to do something. What God does, God does as a Trinity of three Persons together, and yet some actions are specific to each Person. At this point, the human mind goes on overload, and we simply have to let it be that way.

Perhaps the most important thing to keep in mind about God the Father is the word *Father*, which comes to us revealed by God. In fact, the Hebrew word *Jesus* used in referring to the Father is *Abba*, an affectionate term which in Hebrew comes closer to something like *Daddy*.

10 the son: Jesus Christ *(12)*

Catholics (and many other Christians) believe that the Son, the second Person of the Trinity, became a human being. As a human being, he is known as Jesus of Nazareth, or Jesus *Christ*. *Christ* is not a last name like Smith or Jones. It's a Greek word that means the same as the Hebrew word *messiah*, which means *anointed* or *chosen*. Jesus was the fulfillment of God's promises to the Hebrew people to send a messiah to set things straight again between God and human beings. Jesus could do this because he was truly God and truly human at the same time. We say that he was one person with two natures—a divine (God) nature and a human nature.

Since he was truly God and truly human, his conception involved elements of both. Jesus was conceived by the power of the Holy Spirit in the womb of the Virgin Mary, but how it happened is mysterious. As a human being, he was like us in all things except sin. He learned to talk, walk, read, write—all the while, remaining God. The word for this extraordinary and wonderful event is *Incarnation*, which means *coming into flesh*. God took on human nature and therefore a human body.

Christ is not a last name like Smith or Jones.

Why? The simplest answer, one that includes all the others, is simply love—God's overwhelming love for all creatures. But we can break that down into three specific reasons.

First, God the Son became human to save us, to reunite us with God. Sin had created a huge separation between human beings and God. Some repair had to be made to bridge that gap and conquer the power of evil. In sacrificing his life on the cross and rising to new life, Jesus took the sin and guilt of the world upon himself and broke its power. He truly died and truly rose to new life, taking all of us with him both ways. We call this the redemption, which means buying or winning back.

Secondly, Jesus came to reveal God to us in a way we could understand. A common anecdote relays the story of a little girl who asked her mother what God looked like. The mother answered, "No one knows that." The child responded, "They do now"—she had just drawn a picture of God!

In Jesus, we find not what God looks like physically but what God *is* like. How does God think and operate, so to speak? We look at Jesus; we study what he did and said in the inspired words of Scripture. *That's* how God thinks and operates.

Finally, Jesus came to teach us how to respond to God's love and to personally model for us a way of life that leads to everlasting life, a life based on love and service to others.

11 the Holy Spirit *(12–13)*

The Spirit is more difficult to picture or form a concept of than the Father or the Son, Jesus, but let's try this human example. "John and his son Chris are inseparable, so intense is the *spirit of love* between them." That's not too difficult to understand on a human level. Now picture that this love between a Father and a Son is *so intense, so complete,* that it *is a Person.* That's one classic way of "explaining" the Spirit. To use another human example, what makes a loving husband and wife "one"? It's the *spirit* of love, of giving of self that they have for one another.

Think also of things we associate with the word *spirit:* energy, enthusiasm, vitality, power, and even life itself. Those ideas help explain the work of the Spirit among us. The Spirit brings us alive in living the Christian life both individually and as a community or Church. The classic example of this is recorded in the New Testament book of the Acts of the Apostles.

> The Spirit brings us alive in living
> the Christian life both individually and
> as a community or Church.

. . . .

On the feast we call Pentecost, the Spirit came upon the apostles. Acts describes them as transformed from fearful, timid, what-are-we-going-to-do-now believers into strong, confident ones. That transformation usually takes place much more gradually in us, with setbacks and bumps in the road along the way. But if we cooperate with the gifts of the Spirit, it does happen.

The Gifts of the Spirit

The seven gifts of the Holy Spirit are based on Isaiah 11:2-3 and First Corinthians 12:8-10. Sometimes older people think we have added some new ones. Actually, we've simply renamed four of them to make them more understandable for modern times. You may see them listed both ways in different textbooks or other study material, most likely in preparation for the sacrament of confirmation. But they are the same gifts.

TRADITIONAL, OLDER NAME	NEWER NAME
Wisdom	Wisdom
Understanding	Understanding
Counsel	Right Judgment
Fortitude	Courage
Knowledge	Knowledge
Piety	Reverence
Fear of the Lord	Wonder and Awe in the Presence of God

12 salvation and redemption *(13)*

We've already mentioned some basic ideas about salvation and redemption in the section on why God became a human being—namely, that sin had created a huge gap, a distance between God and God's creatures. You might think of it as people being paralyzed through their own actions and unable to respond to God's invitation to eternal life and happiness. Jesus took that paralysis, that guilt, that deathly distance upon himself, freely accepted it, and freely gave his life to repair it.

Jesus identified himself with our sinfulness even though he was sinless himself. Through his earthly death, he experienced the spiritual death that would have permanently been ours and took our place in doing so.

But that's only half of the story. When he rose from the dead, he broke the power that sin and death had over us. As a result, it is again possible for us to live the life God had intended for us from the beginning. This is **redemption**, and we sometimes refer to it with the familiar phrase that Jesus "opened the gates of heaven."

Salvation brings in our part, and here we have to be careful to understand it correctly. Our part is *accepting* this completely free gift of redemption. We do not earn it or deserve it on our own, no matter how many good deeds we perform. It is a free gift that we already have.

God does not say, "I'm going to *make* you accept redemption and eternal life no matter what you do and whether you want it or not!"

What we *can* do, however, is refuse it and throw it away by completely rejecting God through a life of deliberate, serious, continued sin. God created us with free will and God respects it.

God does not say, "I'm going to *make* you accept redemption and eternal life no matter what you do and whether you want it or not!"

We don't always appreciate this gift, this being saved, because we often don't *feel* we were ever in danger of *not* being saved. We're like children born in a town that had been destroyed by a horrendous flood quite some time ago. We hear the story of how someone came along and rebuilt the town for all those who chose to live in it. We're grateful for that in an abstract sort of way. But because we were born and grew up after the flood and we now live in the restored town, we don't always feel the terrible loss and appreciate the radical restoration.

Even though Jesus, historically, died and rose two thousand years ago, redemption is an action of God, who exists outside of time. Redemption/salvation is, for us, a "right now" reality. We need to pray for an understanding of this spectacular, undeserved gift, an understanding that will prompt us to say thanks for it more often and from the heart.

13 grace *(13–14)*

The word *grace* is used in many ways to describe many aspects of our life and relationship with God. One idea is behind all of them: grace is God's *favor*. God looks upon each of us and says, "I really like that person. I'm going to share myself with that person and help him or her." God doesn't have to do this, but God wants to and chooses to. Basically, that's grace.

When you choose someone to be a special friend, for no other reason than that you simply like that person, want to share your life and self with him or her, and want to help him or her in every way you can (even though that person is not perfect), you're extending your grace to that person. God's grace, obviously, is a lot bigger than that—and God chooses to give it to *every* person, not just one special person out of kazillions. To God, each of us is a special, chosen one.

To begin with, God's own life is shared with us. On our own, we can do only things that flow from natural human abilities. We learn to add and subtract, swing a baseball bat, drive a car, and earn an income. If we work at it hard enough, we may accomplish something unusual like climbing Mount Everest. But even something out of the ordinary like climbing Mount Everest is still within the range of purely human abilities. It doesn't qualify us to hang out in heaven. Heaven is *supernatural* because God is there. Heaven requires *God's* life.

> "Doing the right thing" is not something that always comes naturally.

Think of it like this. You can work yourself into the most magnificent physical condition possible, but you still won't be able to live on the sun. It's just plain too hot there. Similarly, on our own, there's no way we can get ourselves into good enough spiritual shape to live in heaven. Only by sharing in God's own life are we able to live there. We call this sharing in God's life **sanctifying grace**.

Doing the right thing is not something that always comes naturally. Unfortunately, doing the wrong thing—sin—sometimes feels perfectly natural. Sometimes an opportunity comes along to do something extra, something especially good, even though it's not a strict obligation, but it seems difficult, perhaps too difficult. At these times, we need help to do what's right, or to accept the challenge to do something especially good.

That help is also grace. We sometimes refer to it as **actual grace**, which means grace that enables us to *act* (not *actual* as opposed to *imaginary*). When a person backs away from sexual activity that shouldn't happen, even though his/her body is full of desire, actual grace is at work. When a parent decides to take his/her children on a Saturday afternoon outing instead of watching TV or taking a nap, actual grace is at work.

14 worship (14)

We use this word so often to describe wrong actions (people "worshiping" money or power; the Israelites who "worshiped" a golden calf) that we can get out of touch with

what it should mean. True worship belongs to God alone. It begins with recognizing the reality of who God is, who we are, and our relationship to God. God is our Creator. We exist only because God, out of love, wants us to exist.

Once we recognize this reality, we do something in response to it. We acknowledge that God is the source of everything, including our very selves. We say so, both in words and in actions. This takes many forms. We worship in public, as a community. The central act of worship in the Catholic faith is the Mass, wherein we celebrate the sacrament of the Eucharist. (More on this later.) We worship in private through individual prayer.

15 sacraments *(14–15)*

Sacraments are supernatural events in which God touches our lives in a special way. The word *sacrament* literally means *sign*. To understand what happens in each sacrament, we look to the sign which literally *is* the sacrament.

Let's back up a bit and think about signs in general. Life is filled with them. They're one of the principal ways in which we get information and learn in general. A green traffic light indicates that a car is allowed to go through an intersection. A diagonal bar drawn across a picture of a cigarette inside a circle warns that smoking is not allowed in that area. A wedding ring is a sign that the person is committed to a spouse in a special loving relationship. A handshake is a sign that the people agree on something. A hug is a sign of friendship, affection, sympathy, or celebration.

Most signs simply give a message. You should bring your car to a stop at this corner; first aid is available here; turn right down this corridor to get to Room 210. But they don't *make the message happen*. A stop sign doesn't bring a car to a halt. A red cross doesn't stop the bleeding from a cut. 210 ➜ doesn't carry anyone to that room.

But—to engage in a bit of fantasy for a moment—what if they did? What if a red light or a stop sign actually brought cars to a halt? We would have a sign that does two things: (1) gives a message and (2) makes that message happen.

Sacraments are that kind of sign. But it's not fantasy. It's spiritual reality. Sacraments cause the message of the sacramen-

■ ■

Most **signs** simply give a **message**.

tal sign literally to happen in the life of a person receiving that sacrament.

Now if a sacrament were simply a *thing*, we would have something close to magic. Faith is not magic, God is not a powerful wizard, and sacraments are not things. Because of the way our language works, we sometimes have to talk about them in ways that sound impersonal. But a sacrament is the action of a person—Jesus—who communicates the supernatural action of Father, Son, and Spirit to us in some specific way. We'll talk about the action of each of our seven sacraments (baptism, confirmation, Eucharist, reconciliation, anointing of the sick, matrimony, and holy orders) in separate sections.

> ➤ **If baptism makes a person a new creation, a child of God, and an adopted heir of heaven, why do some baptized people reject God and raise hell instead?**

Some sacraments, such as baptism, can be celebrated only once. When you're baptized, you're baptized; you can't undo it, and you can't repeat it for greater effect. Others, such as the Eucharist, can be celebrated over and over throughout a Catholic's lifetime.

A common question or doubt is, "Why don't they work better?" If baptism makes a person a new creation, a child of God, and an adopted heir of heaven, why do some baptized people reject God and raise hell instead? Because God respects our free will and because there's a difference between *what we are* and *how we behave.*

Let's use an example from civil life. A person who is sworn in as mayor now *is* the mayor. He or she is expected to work for the good of the city and possesses certain powers to do so. But that doesn't mean he or she will behave that way, or is forced to do so.

He or she may take bribes, embezzle funds, and allow organized crime to infiltrate the city instead.

Similarly—but on a permanent, supernatural level—a baptized person *is* a child of God and adopted heir of heaven. But he or she can choose to act otherwise and throw that inheritance away. We are people, not sacramental robots.

It may seem as though sacraments are an individual affair, a private matter between God and an individual. Not true, even though some can be celebrated privately; reconciliation, for example, is often private. In some way or other, each celebration of a sacrament affects the whole community, the Church.

Think of it like this. Imagine that there's a rather dull party going on—so dull, in fact, that people are beginning to think up excuses to leave, such as needing to review their World Cultures notes from two years ago. Imagine that Jesus enters the gathering and gives one person the ability to tell wonderfully funny jokes, another a beautiful voice, another the skill to make absolutely delicious snacks, and so on.

Would he do this so that the first person could go off in a corner and tell jokes into a tape recorder? The second go home and sing in the shower? And the third make snacks just for him/herself? No, Jesus would touch and empower each of those people so that they could enliven the whole group.

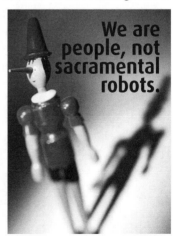

We are people, not sacramental robots.

In a similar way, the grace of each sacrament affects the individual person in a way that not only changes him or her but also has the purpose of working for the spiritual good of the whole community, the Church.

16 baptism *(15)*

The sign of a sacrament tells us what is happening and, in fact, *makes* that happen. Baptism is a fairly complex ritual filled with many signs, but the principal one is water. Although baptism can be celebrated simply by the pouring of water over the head of the person to be baptized, originally—and often today as well—the person is immersed completely in water three times as the baptizing person speaks the words, "I baptize you in the name of the Father, the Son, and the Holy Spirit."

What does that sign of water *say*—and, therefore (because it's a *sacramental* sign), *do*?

Water can cause death, yet it's absolutely essential to life. If you stay beneath water, you die. At the same time, you cannot stay alive without water. Both of these realities—death and life—happen in baptism. You experience the spiritual death that Jesus took upon himself when he physically died on the cross, and you experience the rising to new life, which he accomplished when he rose from the dead. You die to sin and rise to supernatural life.

Water also signifies cleansing. A baptized person is cleansed both from what we call original sin—the great distance between God and human beings—and (in the case of people baptized when they are older) from all personal sins they have committed.

Both of these realities– death and life –happen in baptism.

Baptism of Desire

We enter the life of grace through the sacrament of baptism. Yet it's obvious that millions of people, because of the situations they were born into and in which they grow up, have no real chance to be baptized. Many have never been exposed to the Christian faith in any meaningful way. There are two ways of addressing this situation. One is to conclude, "Gee, what a bad break, but God has no choice; God has to deny salvation. After all, the rules are the rules." The other is to realize that God is not exactly handcuffed by human conditions.

Catholics believe that if someone tries to do what is right in the circumstances in which he or she lives, that person *would want and choose to be baptized* if he or she fully understood what baptism is and does. This is called *baptism of desire* and places that person in the state of grace. As Saint Peter said, "I truly understand that God shows no partiality, but in every nation anyone who fears him and does what is right is acceptable to him" (Acts 10:35).

Similarly, we believe that infants and children too young to understand right from wrong, and who die without being baptized, are somehow given a chance to make a choice for or against God, to accept or reject salvation. Exactly how does God arrange this? That's not our business to figure out. God is God; he can handle it.

17 confirmation *(15–16)*

The sacrament of confirmation completes the action that was begun in baptism with the gift of the Holy Spirit. In New Testament times, the coming of the Spirit upon believers was a separate action from baptism—related to it and built upon it, but separate. It still is. Sometimes confirmation is celebrated immediately after baptism, and sometimes there's an interim of several years.

We return to the sign of the sacrament for an understanding of what is happening. Like baptism, confirmation is a complex ritual, but the essential sign is threefold: anointing with chrism, laying on of hands, and speaking the words, "Be sealed with the gift of the Holy Spirit."

The sacrament of CONFIRMATION completes the action that was begun in baptism with the gift of the Holy Spirit.

Chrism is a blessed, fragrant, oil-like substance, and anointing is an ancient religious ritual. It signifies being chosen and strengthened for a special role. Placing hands upon the head of someone signifies a conferring of power.

A seal indicates a final, confirmed belonging to something or someone (ever hear of a seal of approval?). All of these happen in the sacrament of confirmation.

What role? What power? What belonging? The role of being a fully functioning member of the body of Christ, the Church. The power of God's grace to move from the role of a child to the role of an adult. A confirmed Catholic is now permanently different, just as he or she was permanently different through baptism, but now in a fuller, more mature way.

Who brings this about? The Holy Spirit. Confirmation is often known as "the sacrament of the Spirit." We can understand more of the Spirit's relationship to us by studying the strange and wonderful word which Jesus used in promising us the Spirit:

Paraclete.

It's an exceptionally complex word. No one English word fully conveys its meaning, which is why some Bible translations simply keep the Greek word. Unfortunately, we don't speak Greek, so *Paraclete* doesn't mean much to us until we understand its complex meaning. Take the concepts of advocate, helper, counselor, advisor, teacher, and friend, put them all together in one word, and you have *Paraclete*.

18 reconciliation *(16)*

Imagine that a friend has done something very wrong that hurt you—stole thirty dollars from your purse or billfold. And let's say that, from the circumstances, you know he or she did it; there's no other possible explanation. The truth is that you still like this person. Your friendship together goes back quite a few years. You're willing to start over, but right now, things are awkward, to say the least. Your friend doesn't face the issue with you and—probably out of embarrassed guilt—pretty much avoids you. Starting over, however, is going to take some honest communication.

There's a similarity between that situation and our relationship with God when we've done things that are morally wrong, things we call sin. Pretending that nothing significant ever happened doesn't work. That's what the sacrament of reconciliation is all about: getting what went wrong out in the open so we can deal with it, get rid of it, and move on.

Jesus gave his apostles the power to extend God's forgiveness in person, to give a sign that would make it happen. That's the sacrament of reconciliation. We sometimes call it *confession*, which is accurate for the part of the sacrament in which we admit in words what we did wrong, although that's only part of the sacrament. The sacrament is sometimes also called *penance*, and again that word expresses part of it—doing something to make up for what we did wrong. *Reconciliation*, which means putting a broken or strained relationship lovingly back together, describes the whole experience and reality of the sacrament.

> **Pretending that nothing significant ever happened doesn't work.** ◀

Part of the "Practices" section of this book reviews how to receive the sacrament of reconciliation.

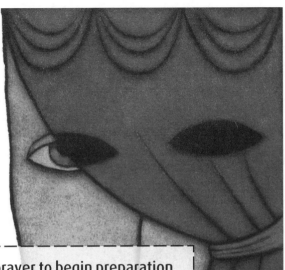

⚓ prayer to begin preparation for reconciliation
(perhaps after a long time)

O God of many, many second chances, hear my prayer of repentance. It's not as good as it could be and should be—the repentance, I mean. It's been too long in coming. I have failed to believe in your boundless mercy, giving up hope in your help to change the patterns of selfishness and sin that threaten to rule me. I ask for the grace to believe fully that you are a God of enduring hope, a God of generous mercy, a God of endless patience, a God of extraordinary compassion and understanding...a God who every minute awaits my response.

AMEN

19 anointing of the sick *(16)*

Anointing of the sick is a sacrament that addresses the needs of a person who is significantly ill, injured, and/or possibly in danger of death. Danger of death is not, however, a needed condition for receiving the sacrament. The basic sign is again an anointing with oil, which signifies healing and strengthening.

There are many types of healing and strengthening. One type occurs when a sick or injured person recovers and regains his/her strength to go on living as he or she did before. And sometimes that is precisely what happens. A nonbeliever, of course, would find it easy to say, "Well, that would have happened anyway; it had nothing to do with faith."

Another kind of healing and strengthening enables someone to accept his/her condition—to overcome discouragement or even resentment over a long-term illness or a permanent condition that restricts the activities he or she used to do and enjoy. Another kind enables someone to rise from spiritual weakness or a not-exactly-close-to-God lifestyle. ("Being in the hospital for two months gave me a lot of time to think about where my life was headed.") Finally, another kind of healing and strengthening enables a person to face the real possibility and prospect of death with peace and trust.

What kind of healing and strengthening is God's call?

The anointing of the sick brings about the healing and strengthening most needed by the person who receives the sacrament and by the whole Church, which is always affected by every individual's life. As to what kind of healing and strengthening happens—that's God's call.

20 matrimony *(17)*

When it comes to sacraments, we see the faith-grace-Jesus connection easily six out of seven times. Baptism, confirmation, Eucharist, reconciliation, anointing of the sick, and holy orders—they all look religious. We have little or no problem hearing that they make Jesus present.

Then there's matrimony. Even though Catholic weddings take place in a church, we sometimes figure that's simply an appropriate place to ask God's blessing. Somehow it's hard for us to believe and appreciate that *marriage does what every other sacrament does: It makes Jesus present here on earth* in a special way. And that's not merely for as long as the wedding ceremony lasts, just as the presence of Jesus at baptism doesn't end when the baptismal ceremony is over.

Every good thing a married couple does, from making love to making car and house payments, makes Jesus present. These are holy actions, no matter how ordinary they may seem. (Jesus himself looked pretty ordinary at the time; that was precisely the problem many people had with him.) The closer a husband and wife become—through sharing themselves emotionally, sexually, and in service to each other—the more they reflect the intense closeness and sharing of the Trinity. The deeper their love becomes, the more they reflect the love of God for the people and of Christ for the Church.

[Marriage] makes Jesus present here on earth in a special way.

This loving presence of Christ is not meant to inspire only them or stay contained within their apartment or house. They have the incredible power and privilege of cooperating with God in creating new life. They're called to make their children feel so loved that when the children hear God loves them immensely, they'll think, "I know what that feels like."

a prayer for my future family

Loving Father, if I am called to the sacramental life of matrimony, hear my prayer now for the person who will be my spouse. Be with her/him today and every day. Help her/him through the challenges of becoming an adult and send my support in prayer through any difficulties. In this way, may I genuinely love this person even before we meet.

I ask for help ahead of time to be respectful and honorable when we meet and begin a relationship. I ask for help ahead of time to be faithful, supportive, strong, and as loving as I can be when we are married.

If I am privileged to help create new human beings, I pray today for my children. You exist outside of time, and you know who they will be, so I can pray for them now. Help me to do everything I can now to become the best parent I can be for them, from the day they are born to the day you call me home to heaven.

AMEN

21 holy orders *(18)*

You may not have thought of yourself as a priest, but all baptized persons share in the priesthood of Christ. The role of a priest is to offer worship to God through the giving of sacrifices, offerings, and gifts to God. Through baptism, all of us are empowered to do this in a basic way.

Public worship, however, requires a leader—someone who leads the community, represents them to God, officially bears the gifts of the community to God, and represents God to the community. Priests of the Jewish faith in the Old Testament offered the animal sacrifices prescribed by the law of Moses.

The gift offered in the Catholic worship we call the Mass is Jesus himself, who then becomes God's gift in return to us. (We'll look at this extensively in the immediately following sections on the sacrament of the Eucharist and on the ritual of the Mass.) This happens through powers given to a man who becomes a priest in a special way in the sacrament of holy orders—the power to consecrate bread and wine so that they become the Body and Blood of Jesus.

> You may not have thought of yourself as a priest, but all baptized persons share in the priesthood of Christ.

Priests exercise other powers and duties within our Catholic community. Priests are empowered to forgive sins in the name of Christ in the sacrament of reconciliation. A priest anoints the person receiving the anointing of the sick. Normally it is a priest who baptizes, although any Christian can baptize an unbaptized person in a danger-of-death emergency.

A deacon, who also receives the sacrament of holy orders, can carry out some of the functions of a priest. Deacons often preside at baptisms and preach homilies.

22 Eucharist *(18)*

All Christians acknowledge Jesus as their Savior. All Christians are baptized. All believe in the Bible as the word of God. We have all these things in common with other Christians (Baptists, Methodists, Lutherans, and so forth). The celebration of the Eucharist, more than anything else, defines us as specifically *Catholic* Christians. The Eucharist is the central sacrament of the Catholic Church and the core of our public worship.

Celebrating the Eucharist goes by other names as well: The Mass, the liturgy, the Lord's Supper, the Sunday celebration, and there are related terms such as holy Communion and the blessed Sacrament. Where did all this begin? In a room somewhere in Jerusalem about two thousand years ago on an evening we now call Holy Thursday in Holy Week. The occasion is what we now call the Last Supper. Jesus was only a few hours away from sacrificing his life on the cross out of love for us.

He wanted to be remembered and to remain with his followers in a special, very close way for all time. More than that, he wanted us to be able to *reenact and celebrate the gift of his life* that he was about to offer for us. He created a way to accomplish exactly that. We call it the Eucharist.

The meaning of the word is important. It comes from the Greek word that means *to return thanks. Return*—that's a *verb*, an *action*. It's something we *do*. We have received a spectacular, totally undeserved gift called salvation from sin and death and the promise of eternal life and perfect happiness. We need to return thanks for that.

Celebrating the Eucharist is the highest form of returning that thanks because in the Eucharist we have a gift truly worthy of God, and that gift is…*God…Jesus*. We reenact the gift that Jesus gave on the cross, the gift of himself. The only difference is that Jesus appears differently. He looks like bread and wine. But after the moment of the Mass we call the consecration, bread and wine become the Body and Blood of Jesus. He is just as present to us in what *only appears to be* bread and wine as he was to Mary and Joseph at their home in Nazareth, just as present as he was to the apostles.

"Take this bread and eat it, for this *is* my body…drink from this cup, for this *is* my blood…" (emphasis added). Jesus said so; those are his words. Catholics believe he meant them just as they stand. "Jesus said so"—that's the beginning of the explanation and practically the end of it, too, unless you want to get involved in a very long philosophical and theological discussion. But even

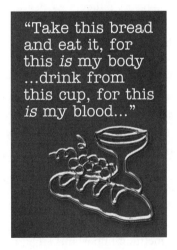

"Take this bread and eat it, for this *is* my body …drink from this cup, for this *is* my blood…"

that won't really explain or prove it. In the Catholic faith, this is called belief in the Real Presence.

Jesus did not have to choose bread and wine for the Eucharist. He could have chosen a rare diamond or a special candle flame. Why bread and wine? Let's think about this *sign* of the sacrament.

They are food. Bread is not baked so it can stay as an intact loaf forever. It's meant to be consumed as food, as nourishment. Wine is not made to stay in containers forever. It's meant to be consumed at special celebrations. By choosing bread and wine as his Real Presence, Jesus was saying that what happens when we eat and share a special meal is what happens when we celebrate the Eucharist.

Food not only gets very close to us, it becomes a part of us. It enables growth, it provides strength and energy, it sustains life.

And usually it is something we share with others in a meal that brings us together. By choosing bread and wine, Jesus tells us that this is what he is doing for us when we celebrate the Eucharist.

When we celebrate the Eucharist, we offer Jesus, the perfect sacrifice, the perfect gift. Then we receive him back, again the perfect gift, as food. That's the Eucharist.

If this is all true—and it is—why are we not totally overwhelmed by it whenever we come to Mass? Again, because God respects our freedom. Jesus didn't make the sky fall when he was preaching in Galilee two thousand years ago or force people to believe he was the Messiah. Many people saw him, listened to him, and then turned away unbelieving or at least unwilling to be changed by what they saw and heard. Others saw, heard, believed, and followed.

It's no different today. That's the nature of freedom and faith.

23 the Mass (18–19)

The word *Mass* comes from a Latin word, *Missa*, which was spoken at the end of the celebration back when official Catholic worship was in Latin. It means something like *dismissal*. Today we hear the same concept in the words of the priest or deacon, "Go in peace, glorifying the Lord by your life."

The word *liturgy* is often used to describe the Mass, although all the sacraments are liturgy. Like *Eucharist*, the meaning of the Greek word *liturgy* tells us something important. *Liturgy* means something that *a community does together.* There are two parts to the Mass: the Liturgy of the Word and the Liturgy of the Eucharist.

You might compare it to a festive family celebration such as we experience at Thanksgiving or Christmas. It begins with greetings, as people arrive and the occasion begins. People talk and listen. They retell and share stories of family history and

Liturgy means something that community does together.

exchange pieces of family advice. They gather around a table and share a very special meal, which deepens their sense of belonging to one another and their sense of unity as a family. True, our human celebrations don't always turn out perfectly according to that ideal script; we're human beings with weaknesses and failings. But it usually comes close. Even when it doesn't, we don't give up on the idea. We don't say, "Last Thanksgiving the turkey got burnt, and Uncle Josh was in a bad mood, so we won't celebrate Thanksgiving anymore."

When we gather for the Mass, we also exchange greetings. They're a little more formal—"The Lord be with you." "And with your spirit." But they're still greetings that say we're glad to be together.

We listen to stories of our family history and pieces of inspiration. On Sunday, we usually hear a reading from the Hebrew Scriptures (Old Testament), a reading from the New Testament (other than the gospels), and then a reading from one of the four gospels. This is the heart of the Liturgy of the Word: God speaking to us through the inspired words of Scripture. Finally comes the homily, in which the celebrant helps us understand the Scripture better and apply it to our lives.

Then we celebrate the Liturgy of the Eucharist in which, as we said before, we offer to God the perfect gift, Jesus, and receive him back as food, God's perfect gift to us.

24 the Catholic Church *(19-20)*

Does it make any difference what church you belong to? Many people would say no, and we've all heard the reasons they give. "All Churches basically believe and do the same things." Well, yes and no. Yes, they have many things in common, but no, they do *not* all believe and do the same things.

Maybe we should back up a step and ask if it makes any difference whether or not you actively belong to *any* church. (Actively belonging is different from simply saying, "I'm Catholic" or "I'm Methodist" or "I'm Lutheran.") Again, we've heard the reasons people give for saying no. "I don't think you have to belong to a church. I think you can talk to God on your own and see God in nature and things like that."

Yes, you can indeed. But if you look at what Jesus did, and what he told his followers to do, it amounted to a lot more than watching a beautiful sunset and thinking, "That is so awesome... there just has to be a God." Just as God called the Israelites

That is so awesome... there just has to be a God.

together into a community, Jesus did the same thing when he fulfilled the promises made to the Israelites and established a New Covenant. He didn't tell his followers, "Go your separate ways and think religious thoughts." He told them to preach the gospel, to baptize, to guard the truth, to heal, to worship together, and to make the love of God visible—in other words, to be an active sign of his continuing presence and work among us. Try getting millions of people to do those things without any organization whatsoever.

In establishing a community, Jesus was building on human

nature. We learn, grow, and receive support—for virtually anything and everything—through other people in communities. (Try learning soccer with nothing but yourself, a soccer ball, and a rulebook…to say nothing of playing it!)

For centuries, Christians were Christians. There were no different Christian *denominations*, as we sometimes call them today. But unfortunately, disunity has crept in, and today there are many different Christian churches. We Catholics have much in common with all of them. We believe in the same one God, we follow Jesus as our Savior, and we accept the Bible as the inspired word of God. We do many of the same works of service, such as striving for social justice and caring for the sick and the poor. That's a great deal to have in common.

Catholics respect the faith of other Christians, as well as the

Church Headquarters

The "headquarters" of the Catholic Church is in Vatican City, which is located in the heart of Rome, Italy. That is one of the reasons we are called Roman Catholics. The buildings that make up this headquarters are usually called the *Vatican,* and they're located within the very small (109 acres!) boundaries of this totally independent city-state. The chief bishop of the Catholic Church lives here. He is known as the pope, which comes from the Italian word for *father,* so we often refer to him as *the Holy Father.* The most recent Church council (1962-1965) met at the Vatican. Councils are named after the place where they are held. This was the second time a council had been held at the Vatican, so it's usually referred to as Vatican II. There have been twenty-one general or ecumenical councils in our two-thousand-year history.

faith of non-Christians. But we do not believe that it all amounts to the same thing—there are no real differences.

The Catholic Church differs from other Christian churches in a number of ways. We are organized differently from most of them in what we sometimes call the *structure* of the Church. We approach and interpret the Bible differently than some other Christian churches do. We have different styles of prayer and we have different religious devotions and practices.

> ▶ We can try to be so respectful of other faiths that we lapse into what we might call *Whateverism*.

What is most distinctively Catholic, however, are the sacred signs and actions we call sacraments, which we've already discussed. We believe that God gave the Church the power to make certain things and actions special channels of the supernatural—the chrism of confirmation, for example, and the bread and wine of the Eucharist. We do not believe that these are simply prayer services containing some religious symbols. We believe that they are the direct, supernatural action of God upon our lives and the life of the community. And so, our central act of worship is not simply Bible readings and a sermon or homily. We include them in our Liturgy of the Word. But then we gather around the table of the Eucharist, offer Jesus in the form of bread and wine, and receive him in return as food.

Asking, "But which Christian church is *right*?" is not a practical question because it assumes that the other Christian churches are wrong. While some Christians unfortunately think this way, most do not, and "We're right—they're wrong" is not the position of the Catholic Church.

At the same time, we can try to be so respectful of other faiths that we lapse into what we might call *Whateverism*. Whateverism says that every faith, every church, is really the same, so it doesn't make any difference. Faith and church membership become a matter of *whatever*.

Catholics believe that the Catholic Church—which has an unbroken, historically provable line of continuing leadership and tradition from the present back to the time of the apostles—*has preserved and teaches the FULLNESS OF THE TRUTH* which Jesus brought us. The last sentence is worth reading again. It's the authentic Catholic outlook on the Catholic Church with regard to other Christian churches. Notice that it doesn't say that Baptists are all wrong, or that Methodists worship false gods. The key idea is in italics above.

Nor do Catholics believe that everything about the Catholic Church is perfect. We believe that the Church is both a divine institution (founded directly by God) and a human institution (filled with and governed by imperfect human beings).

We can be disappointed at imperfections in the Church (just as other Christians are disappointed at imperfections in *their* churches), but imperfections should not lead us to abandon faith. Truth remains truth, even when spoken by a human being with faults and weaknesses. (A math teacher may be an unpleasant person and spend too much time at the racetrack, but two plus two still equals four.)

25 the afterlife: heaven, hell, and purgatory *(20)*

"We're not going to get out of this life alive," someone once quipped, and it's true. Well, sort of. We won't be alive *in the way we are now*. But dead in the sense of totally gone, wiped out forever except in the memory of our immediate descendants? No. Actually, we're very much alive, but in a different manner. Our bodies decompose, but our souls live forever…somewhere. Denying that is denying the promise of

God, the words of Jesus, and the teaching of the Christian faith. Catholics—along with all Christians—believe that there are two final places, or states of existence in the afterlife: heaven and hell.

Heaven. The two big questions are "Who goes there?" and "What's it like there?"

In simplest terms, heaven is promised to those who have made a basic decision and effort to love God and live as God has commanded. Once we pass into the next life, deciding for or against God is a thing of the past, and we are left with the decision we made.

As for what heaven is like, that's impossible to describe in human words for the same reason that it's impossible to fully describe God in human words. Even though we don't always realize it or act like it, God is the total fulfillment and the *only* fulfillment of our desire for happiness. In heaven, we will experience God fully.

Heaven.
The two big questions are, "Who goes there?" and "What's it like there?"

Take an experience that gives you a tremendous rush of wonder, excitement, and joy. For some people, that might be a roller coaster ride shared with people they love, as a celebration of a marvelous event that happened to them. (If you don't like roller coasters, substitute a different experience that for you is filled with wonder, excitement, and joy.) Multiply such an experience several billion times. Even that is a pale, inadequate comparison of what it will be like to *experience God*. This experience will never end. It will be an eternal, nonstop NOW…which is nevertheless ever new and fresh.

Hell. Hell is the opposite—the *total absence* of God. That's more than simply a never-ending, really dull day. Think of a time when you could have had something really nice, like a great grade on a test, or a really satisfying relationship, but you blew it. You chose something else instead, something that you now realize was empty, stupid, and meaningless. Again, multiply that experience several billion times.

One young person used the example of choosing to watch cartoons instead of walking a relatively short distance to pick up a check for several billion dollars…and now the opportunity is gone forever. (Even that's a pale example.) How would that situation feel? "Like hell" is probably a good description.

Purgatory. Catholics believe that a temporary state called *purgatory* exists for people who have left this life in the grace of God but without the complete unselfishness and ability to love required for heaven. Sometimes this is referred to as dying with some "stains of sin" left. Purgatory is a purifying process which cleanses a person of any such stains and enables him or her to enter and take part in the complete loving of heaven.

Hell.
Hell is the opposite— the total absence of God.

You might think of it like this. An athlete reports for the first game of the season but is just not quite ready for the action of the game. He or she is not quite strong enough or limber enough, and does not quite have enough vigor and stamina to function in the game.

At the same time, he or she is not hopelessly beyond getting in shape. So, the coach prescribes an intense conditioning program to bring that person into the shape needed to play in the game. Similarly, we may need a *spiritual* conditioning program to enable us to love perfectly in heaven. That's purgatory. It's another example of God reaching out to heal our weakness. Purgatory is a state of hope, not (like hell) misery and despair.

26 the body of Christ / the communion of saints *(21)*

Paul, writing in the New Testament, searched for an image to describe how close we Christians are to one another in Christ and how interdependent we are on one another. The image he came up with, inspired by God, was a human body with Christ as the head. *That's* close! We may not always feel it or see the effects, but our membership in Christ means we are members of one another. Not just our family and close friends—*all* who are in Christ. We are related and spiritually connected forever.

This concept beautifully describes the purpose and the importance of our differences, our varying gifts. It's very difficult for a kidney to tie a shoelace or give someone a hug, as hands and arms can. But hands and arms can't filter waste products and poisons from the blood as kidneys do. Our individual gifts work for the common good of the body of Christ, just as the individual parts of the human body work for the good of the body as a whole.

Closely related to this is the idea of the communion of saints. The Church that we personally, physically experience is here on earth. But the Church is bigger than that. It includes all those who have gone before us in Christ—everyone in heaven and everyone temporarily in purgatory as well.

We believe that we can help one another. Through prayer and participating in worship, we on earth can help those who are in purgatory. Those in heaven can help us who are still on earth. (When we reach the next life, we may be absolutely stunned to find out that what we thought were just lucky breaks for us here on earth were not random lucky breaks at all. They were the result of Grandma still working, now from heaven, to help make good things happen for us.)

27 Mary (21–22)

It's safe to say that all Christians regard Mary as a very special and wonderful woman, but actual devotion to Mary and certain beliefs about her are pretty much a "Catholic thing." They're also misunderstood among many non-Catholic Christians, and even among some Catholics themselves.

First, let's make clear what Catholics do *not* believe about Mary. We do not consider her equal to God and worship her; worship is reserved for God alone. We do not believe that Mary herself accomplished our redemption. We do not believe that all prayer must go through Mary, and that we cannot pray directly to God.

Catholics believe that Mary was the physical mother of Jesus and that she conceived Jesus through the power of the Holy Spirit while remaining a virgin. To those who might say, "That's biologically impossible," we respond that it's no more impossible than *God becoming a human being.* God, remember, is in charge here, and God can arrange whatever God wants. At the

★ Since Mary is the mother of Jesus, and we are his body on earth, Mary is truly our mother as well and the mother of the Church. ★

same time, when God decided to become a human being, God chose to use a human being's freely given cooperation—Mary's.

Since Jesus, her Son, was and is God in human flesh, we accurately call her Mother of God. This does not mean she existed before God or is more powerful and more important than God.

We believe that Mary remained a virgin throughout her life. We believe that she was born without the alienation from God and tendency to sin which we call *original sin*, and which affects all other human beings. This belief is called the Immaculate Conception. (Notice that it refers to *Mary's* conception, not that of her Son, Jesus.)

We believe that Mary remained sinless throughout her life. This does not mean she was a robot with no free will and could not possibly have chosen to do wrong even if she wanted to. She chose not to sin. To those who might say, "That's not a real human being," we would respond that human beings are not *meant* to sin, in the same way that, for example, basketball players are not *meant* to miss a shot. If a basketball player, not through some kind of magic but through spectacular determination, never missed a shot, would we say that he or she was not a true basketball player? No, we would say that she or he was *the* basketball player of all time.

Finally, we believe that at her death, Mary was taken to heaven *both body and soul.* This doctrine is called the *Assumption of Mary into heaven.* In other words, the reunion of body and soul, which will happen to us at the end of time, was never necessary for Mary.

Since Mary is the mother of Jesus, and we are his body on earth, Mary is truly our mother as well and the Mother of the Church.

practices

28 sacramentals *(23)*

Our lives are filled with special things. If your home caught on fire and you could rescue only a few, carriable items, you would probably choose items whose value to you couldn't be covered by insurance. They might be things like photographs, a piece of jewelry given by a loved one, a secret family recipe which originated with Grandma, a book with a special inscription, a souvenir from a wonderful vacation or a life-changing retreat. These things remind us, and in a sense put us in contact with, special people, places, and experiences.

Our Catholic faith life is filled with things somewhat like that called *sacramentals.* Sacramentals are objects, words, and actions that put us in touch with Christ and with important ideas in our relationship with God. We are body as well as soul. Sacramentals affect our senses and in doing so enrich our life of faith.

The Catholic faith has a treasury of sacramentals, like holy water, blessed candles and incense, blessed medals, the ashes we receive on Ash Wednesday, and the palms we take home on Palm Sunday. Now they're not magic, nor do they take the place of prayer and liturgical worship. You might look upon a sacramental as a charged battery, which has power in it but doesn't make anything happen until it's connected to something. Sacramentals need to be connected to the faith of a believer. For example, holy water used with faith and reverence has the power to rekindle believers' appreciation for their baptism and their desire to resist the temptations of evil.

You might look upon a sacramental as a charged battery, which has power in it but doesn't make anything happen until it's connected to something.

Religious statues, pictures, and other artifacts are not necessarily sacramentals unless they're blessed. But using them, officially blessed or not, as a trigger of inspiration and reflection about faith is *not* the worship of an idol or a "graven image." It's much the same as having family pictures on the wall at home, but in this case, the family is the Church.

29 seasons of the liturgical year *(23–26)*

The story of our redemption is a very big story, and it's difficult to think about every part of it all at once. Besides, we need variety, changes of pace, changes of mood. So, we celebrate different aspects of the redemption story at different times of the year. Each season of the liturgical year has its own mood and its own traditions.

Advent begins the cycle of liturgical seasons. It starts in late November or early December. During Advent we prepare to remember the Incarnation, the coming-of-Christ story, by re-telling the Hebrew Scriptures (Old Testament) that point to it. We also look forward to the Second Coming of Christ at the end of time, when his work of redemption will be finalized.

During the **Christmas season** we remember and celebrate

this Incarnation, God becoming a human being. We reappreciate and treasure the spectacular reality that God is truly *Emmanuel*, which means "God [is] *with* us."

There are two periods of **ordinary time**; the first one comes right after the Christmas season. It's ordinary only in the sense that it doesn't feature a specific focus or theme like the seasons of Advent and Christmas do. But the term can also remind us that living the Christian life often means doing ordinary things well. (*Ordinary* does not mean easy or unimportant!)

Lent begins with Ash Wednesday (late February or early March, depending on when Easter falls) and ends in the early evening of Thursday of Holy Week, the week right before Easter Sunday. We often connect it with giving up something that we usually enjoy or even pamper ourselves with, and there's nothing wrong with that as a form of penance. But Lent really calls for us to purify ourselves of things that shouldn't be in our lives at all, such as laziness that keeps us from regular prayer and worship or self-centeredness that puts our desires above other people's needs. During Lent, we make a special effort to become more spiritually fit in whatever ways each of us needs to do that. Lent is a season of penance. We'll consider penance in detail in the following section. In the meantime, here are the official regulations for Lenten penance.

Abstinence (not eating meat) applies to all Catholics over age fourteen, except in cases of medical need. Fasting (only one full meal, two lighter ones, no snacks) applies to all Catholics aged eighteen through fifty-nine, again with exceptions for medical need. In the United States, Ash Wednesday and Good Friday are days of both fast and abstinence. The other Fridays of Lent are days of abstinence only.

The **triduum** is the shortest period of the year and the most intense in terms of celebrating the central events of our salvation.

It begins on the evening of Thursday of Holy Week and ends on the evening of Easter Sunday. During these days, we solemnly celebrate Christ's gift of himself to us in the Eucharist, his suffering and death, and his rising from the dead. These events are called the paschal mystery.

The **Easter season** begins on Easter Sunday and lasts for fifty days, ending on the feast of Pentecost, the coming of the Holy Spirit upon the apostles. During the Easter season, we celebrate the magnificent reality of our redemption. Thanks to the Risen Jesus, we have gone from doomed to destined—from a spiritual G.P.A. of 0.0 to 4.0.

Just When *Is* Easter?

Christmas is always celebrated on December 25, which obviously is not always a Sunday. Easter is always on a Sunday, but the date changes. You've probably heard people say, "Easter is early (or late) this year," or ask, "When is Easter this year?" Here's how the date of Easter is determined: It falls on the *first Sunday* following the *first full moon* after *March 20*, which is the vernal equinox, when the sun is directly above the equator. Why such a complicated system? It goes way back in history—to the year A.D. 325, to be exact, when a church council determined the method. This date gave the most moonlight to pilgrims traveling both day and night on their way to special places to celebrate Easter. Easter can be as early as March 22 or as late as April 25. This date then determines the date of Ash Wednesday, the beginning of Lent, which is always forty days before Easter. That's why people also say, "Ash Wednesday is early (or late) this year."

The second period of **ordinary time** is the longest season of the liturgical year—from the Monday after Pentecost to the Saturday before the first Sunday of Advent, when the cycle begins again. It's similar to the first ordinary time, except that it features some great individual celebrations, such as the Feast of the Body and Blood of Christ in June and the Feast of the Assumption of Mary on August 15.

30) penance (26)

If someone deliberately smashes a piece of your property, perhaps out of anger or jealousy, you can genuinely forgive that person and want to rebuild the relationship you may have with him or her. But there's more to the situation than that. The person needs to replace the destroyed property if at all possible. If it's not possible, he or she needs to do *something* to repair the relationship, to make up for the harm and damage that was done. He or she also needs to work on overcoming the tendency to feel jealous and act in anger as a result.

This is sometimes called *making amends*. In religious terms, it's called doing penance or making atonement. The Catholic faith takes it very seriously. Penance can take many forms. One traditional way is the giving up of certain kinds or amounts of food (see *Lent*, previous section). We can give up or limit, at least for a certain period of time, other pleasurable things such as television and other forms of entertainment. Adding times of prayer or lengthening existing

> Three traditional forms of penance— prayer, fasting, and almsgiving (giving money)— can sometimes be accomplished together.

ones is another form of penance. So is giving money that might have been spent on ourselves.

Three traditional forms of penance—prayer, fasting, and almsgiving (giving money)—can sometimes be accomplished together. An example would be "fasting" from watching DVDs over the weekend, spending some of that time in prayer instead, and giving away the money that would have been spent on buying or renting them.

31 receiving reconciliation *(26–27)*

Some Catholics, especially if they haven't received reconciliation regularly, worry about doing it right in terms of what to say or do at what time. There is a standard format, but what goes on inside your heart before and during reconciliation is much more important than any set of memorized words.

Begin with a prayer to make the experience of reconciliation meaningful. Use your own words and/or thoughts. Then do an examination of conscience. That means thinking back over your life since the last time you received reconciliation and remembering the things you have done wrong.

Things that are seriously wrong and/or which tend to keep you distant from God, more than anything else, deserve special attention. Be as thorough and honest as you can without being obsessed about remembering every small detail.

Whether you confess your sins anonymously behind a screen or in person face-to-face with the priest, enter the confessional or reconciliation room. The priest will greet you. Return the greeting, and make the Sign of the Cross. The priest will invite you in some way to trust in God's mercy. Respond with "Amen." Tell how long it has been since your last confession. (If you are returning to confession after quite some time, come as close as you can, again without being obsessed over *the exact* number of months, weeks, or even years.) Confess your sins in a spirit of honesty and sorrow for them, but also with the expectation of the forgiveness that Jesus promised.

The priest may then give you any necessary advice and answer any questions you may have. This is the time to bring them up if you do. He will assign you a penance to help atone for your sins. Frequently it is a set of familiar prayers to say, but it may be something more specifically in

...what goes on inside your **heart** before and during reconciliation

is much more important than any set of memorized words.

sync with a particular sin. He will ask you to make an Act of Contrition. The words to an Act of Contrition are sometimes posted in the confessional area. One form is printed in the "Prayers" section of this handbook. The priest will pronounce the official words of sacramental forgiveness, to which you answer "Amen." Finally, there will be some words of dismissal, such as, "Give thanks to the Lord, for he is good."

32 receiving Communion *(27)*

In the past, regulations for receiving Communion were quite strict, and the procedure was far more formal. Catholics often or even usually attended Mass *without* receiving Communion. The regulations and formalities were a bit much, but they did convey the idea that receiving Communion is not just another automatic, routine thing that Catholics do. We

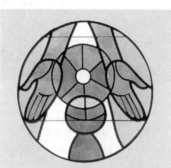

should not think of it that way today, even though the rules for the Communion fast have been relaxed. Receiving Communion is receiving within ourselves the actual Body and Blood of Jesus. That is never routine, small stuff.

To receive Communion, a Catholic must be in the state of grace, that is, not alienated from God by serious sin; must have the right intention ("because everybody else does" is not a right intention); and must have observed the Communion fast. The latter means not eating anything or drinking any liquid other than water for one hour before receiving Communion. Exceptions are made, obviously, for those who are sick or infirm with age or who must take medication.

> To receive Communion, a Catholic must be in *the state of grace*, that is, not alienated from God by serious sin; must have the right intention; and must have observed the Communion fast.

Receiving Communion
"In the Old Days"

The Communion Fast began at midnight and included everything—even water! Catholics approached the *Communion rail,* a marble or wooden divider between the sanctuary and the benches or *pews* in the larger section of the church. They ascended one or more steps, knelt on the top one, placed their hands under a cloth, which was draped over the rail, and formed a flat space in the cloth with their thumbs and forefingers (to hold the consecrated host if it should slip from their tongue.) The priest approached each person from the right, accompanied by an acolyte or *altar server*, who carried a small plate called a *paten*, which was placed under the person's chin (again, to catch the host if it should slip). The priest would hold up the host in front of each communicant and say, in Latin, *"Corpus Domini nostri Jesu Christi custodiat animam tuam in vitam aeternam,"* which means, "May the Body of our Lord Jesus Christ preserve your soul unto eternal life." Then he would place the host on the person's tongue and move to the next person. Only priests were allowed to distribute Communion. If there were many receiving Communion and only one or two priests, the distribution could take...quite some time.

Too much ceremony and too many precautions based on fear? Perhaps. But it did instill reverence for the sacredness of receiving Communion. It was difficult to think of receiving Communion as ordinary and routine.

33 holy days of obligation *(27)*

Catholics are expected to celebrate these special feasts by participating in the Mass, even though they may not fall on a Sunday. With the exception of Hawaii (see below), there are six:

✠ Mary, Mother of God ~ January 1
✠ Ascension ~ the Thursday forty days after Easter
✠ Mary's Assumption ~ August 15
✠ Feast of All Saints ~ November 1
✠ Mary's Immaculate Conception ~ December 8
✠ Christmas ~ December 25

When these feasts fall on a Sunday, there is no obligation to attend Mass more than once. When January 1 (the solemnity of Mary, Mother of God), August 15 (the solemnity of the Assumption), or November 1 (the solemnity of All Saints) falls on a Saturday or a Monday, there is no obligation to attend Mass beyond the normal Sunday celebration. December 8 (Immaculate Conception) and December 25 (Christmas) are always holy days of obligation.

In some areas, in order to enable Catholics whose work makes it genuinely impossible to attend Mass on these days, the local bishop has transferred the celebration of the feast to the following Sunday.

The Ascension is celebrated either the fortieth day after Easter or replaces the seventh Sunday after Easter. Check with your local Catholic Church to know which day applies in your area.

In Hawaii, Christmas and the Immaculate Conception are the only two holy days of obligation (by decree of the Bishop of Honolulu dated March 23, 1992).

34 the corporal (material or physical) works of mercy *(28–29)*

In both the corporal and the spiritual works of mercy (see next section), the word *mercy* doesn't mean taking it easy on someone you could give a hard time to. It means reaching out to others with compassion, understanding, and a desire to help. The works of mercy are not the responsibility only of "official" people in the Church, such as priests, missionaries, chaplains, teachers, and counselors. True, it's a hospital chaplain's official duty to visit the sick, but that doesn't mean the rest of us have no opportunity to do that.

Here are the seven corporal works of mercy, along with some concrete ways of doing them:

◼▮❚▮ **Feed the hungry. Give drink to the thirsty.**
❚▮❚▮ Take part in the school's canned-food drive; contribute to organizations that work to relieve poverty; contribute to disaster- and famine-relief funds; serve meals at a soup kitchen; make a meal for the family or pack lunches for younger siblings; fill someone's plate or pour a glass of milk for someone at the meal table. (Nothing says the hungry or the thirsty have to be living in poverty or facing starvation.)

◼▮❚▮ **Clothe the naked.** Work for a used-clothing
❚▮❚▮ drive; donate your own outgrown but usable clothing; adopt one or more people from an Advent Giving Tree (the gift requests frequently are for needed clothing); help sort donated clothing at a Saint Vincent de Paul site.

◨‖◨ Visit those in prison. Donate books and toys to ◨‖◨ organizations that help the children of prisoners; contact a local prison chaplain for ideas on how you could reach out anonymously to prisoners through the making of cards, seasonal decorations, or small gifts.

◨‖◨ Shelter the homeless. Again, contribute to ◨‖◨ poverty- and disaster-relief agencies and programs; work with Habitat for Humanity to build affordable homes; volunteer at an agency that repairs, cleans, and brightens homes for people unable to do so themselves or that rehabs old buildings to make them habitable and affordable for low-income families.

◨‖◨ Visit the sick. Send a note to a sick or injured ◨‖◨ classmate or organize the making of a card from the class; visit a grandparent or other relative who isn't feeling well, whether in person (recommended if possible), by telephone, or by mail; help an ill younger sibling with homework sent or called in by a classmate; take notes and make needed copies for a classmate who is absent due to illness.

◨‖◨ Bury the dead. Attend the visitation and/or the ◨‖◨ funeral of a relative or the relative of a friend; send a sympathy card, perhaps with an added personal note; make a meal, run errands, or otherwise help those who have suffered the loss of a loved one; take notes and make needed copies for a classmate who is absent due to a death in the family.

35 spiritual works of mercy (29–30)

Admonish the sinner. Show the right path by your own example. Refuse to take part in activities that are wrong; extend a sincere (but not superior and preachy) "I'm worried about you" message to a friend who's getting into drinking, drugs, or other harmful activity.

Instruct the ignorant. *Ignorant* has nothing to do with ability or personality! It simply means those who do not know something that would benefit them to know. Help a younger sibling practice math facts, do homework or research, or complete a school project; help a classmate in a subject you understand better than he or she does; help someone prepare for a test or exam; teach a skill you have to anyone who wants to learn; help coach a team of younger children.

Counsel the doubtful. Give good advice (when appropriate and, usually, when it's asked for) to friends who are unsure what to think or do; support parents, siblings, and friends in making difficult decisions.

Comfort the sorrowful. Express sympathy and support to anyone who has lost anyone or anything—a loved one to death, a relationship, a good grade on a test, a hoped-for scholarship, a role in the school play, a spot on the team roster; console anyone who is going through a difficult time for whatever reason.

◪‖◪ Bear wrongs patiently. Forgive all injuries.
◪‖◪ The person you're reaching out to in this case may not appear to be the needy one because it's someone who has hurt *you,* and you may feel *you're* the one in need! Realize that, although it's possible the person may literally have a mean streak, it's also possible that he or she is acting out of some hurt that you do not know about (and perhaps no one does). This does not mean leaving yourself open to being constantly abused and accepting the abuse. Physical or sexual abuse and ongoing verbal abuse needs to be reported and stopped. But avoid making and implementing plans for revenge.

◪‖◪ Pray for the living and the dead. Chances are
◪‖◪ you enjoy helping others whenever it's possible. Not all the works of mercy, both corporal and physical, are possible at all times, but this one is. There's almost no time when it can't be done! Whether you have a half hour, a half minute, or just a few seconds, you can pray for anyone you choose, including people you don't even personally know, such as the people who were injured in a car accident you heard or read about. You can pray for people who are in a particular situation, such as any young person who is thinking about running away or anyone who is about to commit a life-changing crime. God knows who they are even though you don't. You can even pray for the person who may become your spouse (again, God knows who he or she is) and even (since God exists outside of time) for your own future children (God knows who they will be).

SeCtioN ThrEE

prayer
and some traditional prayers

36 what prayer is *(31–32)*

Prayer is communicating with God. Sounds simple, and it is, but then *simple* doesn't always mean *easy.*

Notice the words *communicating with.* That's broader than *talking to.* Like any conversation with anybody, prayer involves talking and listening. We sometimes skip that second part.

Any conversation you have with another person is going to be colored by two things: how you see yourself and how you see the other person. Prayer is no different. If you see yourself as pretty much in control of everything, you may not feel the need for prayer as much as if you feel weak and helpless. If you feel that you're kind of dirty and unpresentable due to things you've done wrong, you may feel that God is pretty ticked off and not exactly in a great mood to listen to you.

> Like any conversation with *anybody,* prayer involves talking and listening.

You are a child of God, and God is in charge of the drama of your life, even if it seems like you're doing a great job of running that show by yourself at the moment.

So, especially if prayer seems difficult or unappealing, take a little inventory of how you see yourself—or, perhaps more to the point, how you're seeing yourself right now. Then take a look at how you're seeing or feeling about God right now.

If need be, remind yourself of a couple things that never change. You are a child of God, and God is in charge of the drama of your life, even if it seems like you're doing a great job of running that show by yourself at the moment. You're likewise a very *lovable* child of God, and you don't stop being lovable to God no matter how many mistakes you make.

When you pray, you talk—honestly. (Why hold anything back from someone who already knows the whole truth?) You listen—with an open mind and heart. (Why close your mind and heart to the truth and the best advice you'll ever get?)

That's prayer. Ten thousand books on prayer can effectively build on that foundation, but that's still the foundation.

37 why pray? *(32)*

We could subdivide the reasons for prayer into the dozens or hundreds, but they would all fit somehow into one of two main reasons: we *ought* to and we *need* to.

Ought. God gave us life, our very existence. God saved us from eternal death and doom. God continues to keep us in existence, is the source of every good thing we have, supplies the strength to get through hard times, forgives us when we sin, and promises us eternal life and happiness. To say the very least, it just isn't right to accept all those things but never or seldom acknowledge them or the one who gives them to us.

Need. Maintaining and deepening a relationship with anybody requires communication. We have to spend time on it, or it fades and eventually disappears. A relationship with God is no different—from our standpoint. God never changes, never grows weak or indifferent in God's love for us, never stops wanting to care for and help us. But on our end, without the communication of prayer, we can reach a point

Prayer is not always rewarding and fulfilling, but it often is for people who work at it.

where God just isn't important anymore. We may *say* that God is important because it's the official, "right" answer; but we spend time with people who are truly important to us.

Actually, there's a third reason (besides "ought to" and "need to") which speaks to many people. It's **"want to."** Prayer is not *always* rewarding and fulfilling, but it often is for people who work at it. "Work at it" may seem to be the wrong words to use about prayer, but they're not. Few things in life come totally easily and automatically, but we "work at" them (including relationships) anyway. Learning a sport or acquiring some other skill is not always thrilling until we gain some experience at it and learn how to do it, how to develop our particular, personal style at it. Prayer is no different.

38 types of prayer (32–33)

Praise and adoration. God is God—awesome and wonderful. We should say so. Why—because otherwise God wouldn't know and might feel a little down? No, we praise and adore God because it's right and because, well, God likes to hear it in the same way that you will enjoy hearing your children tell you that you're a good mom or dad.

Thanksgiving. Every good thing we have is from God. We need to say thanks. It's just the right thing to do. Thanking God for the good things in our life makes us realize and appreciate them even more.

Petition. There's nothing wrong with asking God for things that will make our lives better. God *likes* to give us good things. However, we don't always have the clearest vision of what is genuinely good for us and will truly make our lives better. In that respect, we're like little children. A shiny, double-edged, razor-sharp knife may look like a really fun and harmless toy to a young child, but a parent who gives it just because the child asks for it is a very weak-brained parent. God is not a weak-brained parent. So sometimes God answers a prayer of petition with "no."

Reparation or contrition. We make mistakes, we sin. (If we don't believe that, we're not in touch with reality.) We ought to and need to say we're sorry. Expressing sorrow for sin is one of the best ways of avoiding it in the future.

Prayer Starters

 With a little imagination, *anything* can be a prayer starter, often for several types of prayer. Sure, gorgeous sunsets will work wonderfully, but let's take something as plain and unexciting as a real estate ad: "Westwood, three-bedroom ranch, many extras, price reduced." *Price reduced* may mean that the owners really need to sell quickly. We can pray that this happens and that they still receive a fair price. We can pray that the owners will be happy wherever they're moving to, and that the people moving in will be happy there. We can pray for people who are homeless, and thank God for having shelter ourselves, whatever it may be. We can tell God we're sorry for times when we envied people who live in a bigger or more modern home with more luxuries. We can pray for construction workers that they may be safe on the job. We can praise and thank God for giving us the ability to design homes of both practicality and beauty.

All from a small real estate ad. Try your prayerful imagination on a bar of soap, a cloud, the sound of a child laughing or crying, a trash can, a truck, a DVD player, a cell phone, a double cheeseburger, a chalkboard, the sound of a siren, the scent and texture of a clean towel, a calculator, a computer.

You can pray with set words that you learn by heart or read from a book or prayer card, with your own words, or sometimes simply with feelings that you open up and direct silently toward God. Investigate different prayer styles or methods and learn what works for you. As for which style is the best, the answer is probably the same as the answer to the question, "What kind of exercise is best?" Answer: the one you'll stay with and actually do. It's okay, however, if your method or style of prayer changes as you grow and change. It's also okay if you find yourself returning to styles of prayer that you used in the past and then drifted away from.

39 prayer to Mary and the saints *(34)*

Prayer to Mary, the greatest of saints, and to other saints is again "a Catholic thing," which non-Catholic Christians may misinterpret. It is *not* that they can make something happen which God cannot or that God is unwilling to grant unless the saints bug him. It's *not* that this takes the place of prayer to God, and once again, it is definitely *not* worship.

It's based on the fact that, by God's design and will, we followers of Jesus are a family. We are spiritually connected, and we can help one another. In fact, helping one another on the journey to heaven is precisely what God wants. God chooses to let people in on the work of one another's journey to heaven, just as a parent will let his or her children help with putting together a swing set that all will enjoy and be delighted by their doing so.

...helping one another on the journey to heaven is precisely what God wants.

That's why we pray for one another. This desire and ability to help one another spiritually doesn't end when some of us enter the next life. (Do you think Grandma will stop caring about you just because she can no longer physically bake you cookies or give you advice face to face?) We are still connected in that wonderful family called the communion of saints. So, asking a saint to pray for you and help you is not all that different from asking someone here on earth to do the same thing.

Big Bro, Big Sis, and Patron Saints

Prayer to the saints is like having a household of big brothers and sisters who are eager to help you. Many of them have experience with special problems and challenges and can help you with similar ones. To begin, you may have been named after a particular saint. That's a good start. ("Dear Saint Cuthbert: That's my name, too, and with a name like that, we've got to stick together.") If you think you've let Jesus down in a major way, talk to Saint Peter, who denied even knowing Jesus. If you do something good but rather strange and get called crazy for doing so, talk to Saint Joan of Arc; she knows a lot about that. Need to put up some drywall? Ask Saint Bartholomew; he's the patron saint of plasterers, but he's probably familiar with the modern version, too. Need help with your soccer skills? Talk to Saint Sebastian, patron of athletes. If you're thinking of joining the military, you can get lots of support. Saints George, Adrian, Michael, Ignatius of Loyola, Sebastian, Martin of Tours, and Joan of Arc are all patrons of soldiers. Saints Catherine of Alexandria, Gregory the Great, Ursula, and John the Baptist de La Salle can all support you in becoming a teacher. Saint Anthony, of course, is well known for being able to help you find lost items. And victims of sexual abuse can talk to Saint Maria Goretti; she'll know what they're talking about.

40 traditional prayers *(34)*

Traditional prayers that you have memorized or can easily find are a comfortable way to begin or end a time of prayer or simply to use on their own. They're like old prayer-friends. The words express some of the most common prayer-thoughts we have. You can develop the meaning of those words by saying them slowly and meditating on them, and you can color them with your own particular feelings or needs at the time you say them. The following sections offer some of the most common in our Catholic heritage.

Amen, which concludes most prayers, is a Hebrew word meaning something like truly or really.

Some of the prayers still include old-fashioned language in just a few places, such as *thou* (you) and *thy* (your), because most Catholics learned them that way, and we've become so accustomed to it that we sometimes stumble over the modern replacements!

Amen, which concludes most prayers, is a Hebrew word meaning something like *truly* or *really*. It expresses wholehearted acceptance of what has just been said.

---

41 the Sign of the Cross

In the name of the Father, and of the Son, and of the Holy Spirit. Amen.

The Sign of the Cross is most often used to begin and/or end prayers, but it can be a prayer all its own, especially when said slowly. It can be used to dedicate an activity to the glory of God.

42 Our Father *(35)*
(the Lord's prayer)

Our Father, who art in heaven, hallowed be thy name; thy kingdom come; thy will be done on earth as it is in heaven. Give us this day our daily bread; and forgive us our trespasses as we forgive those who trespass against us; and lead us not into temptation, but deliver us from evil. (For the kingdom, the power, and the glory are yours, now and for ever.) Amen.

This is a prayer both of praise and of petition. *Hallowed* means *holy and respected*. *Trespasses* refers to sins. *Our daily bread* includes all the things we truly need.

43 Hail Mary

Hail, Mary, full of grace. The Lord is with thee. Blessed art thou among women, and blessed is the fruit of thy womb, Jesus. Holy Mary, Mother of God, pray for us sinners, now and at the hour of our death. Amen.

The first two sentences are taken from the words of the angel Gabriel to Mary. The words of Mary's cousin Elizabeth (mother of John the Baptist) to Mary make up the third sentence. It, too, is a prayer of praise and of petition.

44 the Glory Be
or prayer of praise to the trinity

Glory be to the Father, and to the Son, and
to the Holy Spirit; as it was in the beginning,
is now, and will be forever. Amen.

An older version adds *world without end* after *forever*. That
simply reinforces the idea of *forever*.

- -

45 Mary's rosary

The rosary begins with the Apostles' Creed and
then incorporates the above three prayers. It com-
bines two types of prayer, often called *vocal* (spoken out loud or
with silent lip movement) and *mental* (meditative thoughts). As
we say the above prayers, we think about key events in the lives
of Jesus and Mary called *mysteries*. There are three traditional
sets of mysteries and a fourth, very recent one, formulated by
Pope John Paul II. It's okay if your mind moves back and forth
between the actual words of the prayers and the mystery you're
thinking about or concentrates more on one than the other.

The Joyful Mysteries

1. The Annunciation (Gabriel announces to Mary
   that she is to be the Mother of the Messiah.)
2. The Visitation (Mary visits and helps her cousin,
   Elizabeth.)
3. The Nativity (Mary gives birth to Jesus.)
4. The Presentation (The infant Jesus is presented
   to God in the Temple according to Jewish law.)
5. The Finding in the Temple (Mary and Joseph locate
   Jesus, whom they thought was lost.)

The Sorrowful Mysteries

1. The agony in the Garden (Jesus feels anguish over his coming suffering and death.)
2. The scourging at the pillar (Jesus is brutally whipped.)
3. The crowning with thorns (Jesus is painfully mocked by Roman soldiers.)
4. The carrying of the cross (Jesus makes his way to the hill of execution.)
5. The crucifixion (Jesus dies for our sins.)

The Glorious Mysteries

1. The Resurrection (Jesus rises from the dead.)
2. The Ascension (Jesus is taken to heaven.)
3. The Coming of the Holy Spirit (The Spirit comes upon the apostles at Pentecost.)
4. The Assumption (Mary is taken into heaven both body and soul.)
5. The Coronation (Mary is crowned queen of heaven and earth.)

The Luminous Mysteries (Mysteries of Light)

1. The baptism of the Lord
2. The wedding feast at Cana (Jesus performs his first sign, and the apostles believe in him.)
3. The preaching of the kingdom of God and the call to conversion
4. The Transfiguration of the Lord (The glory of God shines in the face and garments of Jesus.)
5. The institution of the Eucharist

46 the Apostles' Creed

*I believe in God, the Father almighty,
Creator of heaven and earth, and in Jesus
Christ, his only Son, our Lord, who was
conceived by the Holy Spirit, born of the
Virgin Mary, suffered under Pontius Pilate,
was crucified, died and was buried; he
descended into hell; on the third day he
rose again from the dead; he ascended into
heaven, and is seated at the right hand of
God the Father almighty; from there he
will come to judge the living and the dead. I
believe in the Holy Spirit, the holy catholic
Church, the communion of saints, the
forgiveness of sins, the resurrection of the
body, and life everlasting. Amen.*

A creed is a list of the central things we believe, and saying the creed is a prayer, an act of faith. There are two principal creeds in our Catholic heritage—the Apostles' Creed above and the Nicene Creed, or Profession of Faith, which is the one we usually say at Mass. They do not list opposite things, but they are slightly different, and the Nicene Creed is slightly longer.

47 Act of Contrition

My God, I am sorry for my sins with all my heart. In choosing to do wrong and failing to do good, I have sinned against you whom I should love above all things, and against your Church. I firmly intend, with your help, to do penance, to sin no more, and to avoid whatever leads me to sin. Amen.

There are several versions of an act of contrition. Any one of them, or one you make up with your own words which express the above ideas, is a good act of contrition and is suitable for reconciliation and as a prayer at the end of the day.

48 Stations of the Cross

These are a traditional devotion during Lent, but the Stations of the Cross (or Way of the Cross) can be prayed at any time of the year. Traditionally, we walk around the church from one station to the next (some artifact on the church walls will mark each one), or a prayer leader will walk on behalf of a group that is praying the stations. At each station, we think of the event and pray a brief prayer, either from a stations booklet (there are many) or one of our own.

At each station, we think of the event and pray a brief prayer...

1. Jesus is condemned to death on the cross.
2. Jesus accepts his cross.
3. Jesus falls the first time.
4. Jesus meets his sorrowful mother.
5. Simon of Cyrene helps Jesus carry his cross.
6. Veronica wipes the face of Jesus.
7. Jesus falls the second time.
8. Jesus meets the women of Jerusalem.
9. Jesus falls the third time.
10. Jesus is stripped of his garments.
11. Jesus is nailed to the cross.
12. Jesus dies on the cross.
13. Jesus is taken down from the cross.
14. Jesus is placed in the tomb.

Recent versions of the Stations add a fifteenth station, *the Resurrection*, or at least conclude with a closing prayer that recalls the Resurrection. This reminds us that, even when we are concentrating on the suffering and death of Jesus, we must remember that they are incomplete without the Resurrection.

49 morning offering *(36)*

There are several versions of the morning offering, a prayer in which we give our day to our Lord.

Jesus, I will be thinking, feeling, saying, and doing many things today. Some will be happy, and some will be sad. Some will be exciting, and some will be ordinary. I want them all to count. I want them to make a difference for somebody somewhere, to help build your Kingdom here on earth. You have told us that all of us are connected; we are your Body, and we can help each other. I believe that. So I give my day to you right now, ahead of time. When you give yourself to the Father in the Eucharist today, take this day of mine with you, join it to yourself, and let it be a force for helping good things happen throughout the world. Amen.

■ ■

50 Prayer for the Faithful Departed (those who have died)

Eternal rest grant unto them, O Lord, and let perpetual light shine upon them. May their souls and the souls of all the faithful departed, through the mercy of God, rest in peace. Amen.

If this prayer is being said for a particular person, the words *them* and *their* are replaced with *her* or *him* and *his*.

51 Prayer to the Holy Spirit

Come, Holy Spirit. Fill the hearts of your faithful, and make the fire of your love burn within them. Send forth your spirit and there shall be another creation. And you shall renew the face of the earth. O God, you have instructed the hearts of the faithful by the light of the Holy Spirit. Grant that through the same Holy Spirit we may always be truly wise and rejoice in his consolation. Through Christ our Lord. Amen.

The older version of this prayer that you may hear uses slightly different words but expresses the same thoughts. It's an excellent prayer for guidance in making a decision.

52 litanies

A litany is a prayer usually recited with a prayer leader saying the first part of each invocation and others making a repeated response. For example, in the body of the Litany of the Saints, the leader will call the saint's name, and the group responds "Pray for us." Depending on the litany, other responses include "Have mercy on us" and "Lord, save your people."

There are dozens of wonderful litanies in our Catholic tradition, available in prayer books and even online. The Litany of the Saints and the Litany of the Blessed Virgin are two of the most popular, and there are several versions of each. Although the structure of a litany is geared for a prayer leader and a group, you can easily pray them by yourself, taking both parts.

If/When It's Hard to Pray

Sometimes prayer just wells up within us and spills out of us easily and fervently, and we feel great about it. This can happen at a retreat, for example, or at an emotionally charged time of our life. It would be nice if prayer were always like that, but it isn't. There are many times when we literally have to work at it. That shouldn't surprise us. We have to work at almost everything else we do in life. We don't hit home runs the first several times we have a bat in our hands or even every time we swing long after we've acquired some skill. Many saints, even after years of holy living, experienced times when praying felt like trying to move a rock that would barely budge. That's okay. The effort counts anyway.

Quick, short prayers in the midst of busy or stressful situations are good, but we deeply need quiet times of extended prayer. *Extended* doesn't have to mean a half hour. It can mean "a good bit longer than my usual," and *that* could mean as little as ten minutes or even five. At those times, it's important to *prepare* for prayer. We prepare for almost every other significant thing. We study for tests, dress for dates, and warm up before sports. A few moments of quiet, slow breathing, perhaps with the eyes closed, can work wonders in getting prayer off to a good start.

.007 isn't much of anything, except in James Bond movies. Can you afford that much of your day for quiet, deliberate prayer? That's ten minutes. (Actually, it's only .0069444; we rounded up.)

Catholic moral issues
(life in the real world)

53 moral behavior and the life of faith *(37)*

"If I do everything right and never sin, or hardly ever, I'll be saved." Wrong attitude. That makes salvation something we *earn* by how we act. Salvation is a free gift. In the past, some Christians tended toward this attitude and lived in serious fear that they would make God furious. (They also tended to regard almost anything enjoyable as sinful.)

Today, the opposite is more common: "Jesus saved us, and besides, God loves us and forgives everything anyway—so what I do doesn't make all that much difference, at least not when it comes to salvation." That's also wrong. It says that you can call all your own shots—in a sense, be your own god—and it won't matter to God.

The Catholic approach to morality (right and wrong) is not based on a picture of a God who says, "I'm watching for every slightest mistake you make!" Neither is it based on a picture of a God who says, "Oh, well, it doesn't really matter" about whatever we do. Jesus saved us from sin, but he didn't teach that it doesn't exist or doesn't matter anymore.

Salvation is a free gift.

It comes down to this: We need to *act* like the creatures we *are*—children of God, reborn in baptism, and members of the body of Christ. Otherwise, we're saying, in effect, "Of *course* I *believe*—I just don't want to *act* like it."

54 temptation *(37)*

Temptations are urges to do things we know are wrong. They can come from inside ourselves (feelings and desires) or from outside ourselves (suggestions from friends or messages from the media, for example). Three things about temptations are important to remember.

First, temptations are *not* sinful. No matter how strong they are, no matter how often they arise, and no matter how wrong or disgusting the action they suggest, they are not wrong by themselves. Only an *action* or a lack of action, physical or mental, can be right or wrong.

> Becoming aware of a serious temptation is the same as sensing you're in a dangerous situation.

Second, they are not to be taken lightly. If given in to, they lead to actions that *are* wrong—and sometimes life-changing. Becoming aware of a serious temptation is the same as sensing you're in a dangerous situation. You put up your guard, and you get yourself out of the situation as soon as you can.

Third, it's possible (not to mention dumb) to deliberately expose ourselves to temptation, especially one that we *know* is difficult to resist. Visiting, even briefly, a pornographic Internet site, going to an activity that we know will be drug-ridden, hanging out with people that we know are prone to violence—this is inviting temptation into our lives.

That makes about as much sense as an alcoholic who deliberately goes to a bar to drink a soda, hopes that nothing bad will happen, and later says, "I couldn't help it—I was surrounded and overwhelmed by temptation."

55 sin *(38)*

Sin is any deliberate violation of a moral law—a commandment given by God. Sin could also be described as a failure to love or as putting oneself above God.

A sin can be a physical action or a purely mental action. (You can deliberately plan an armed robbery or a murder without moving a muscle; that's sinful, even if you never get a chance to carry it out.) A sin can likewise be a lack of action or failure to act, such as not coming forth with information of a crime that you know and have an obligation to tell.

In traditional Catholic morality, a **mortal** sin is something so serious that it totally destroys our relationship with God. It fundamentally rejects God. Less serious sins are called **venial** sins. It's worth noting that it's probably easier to *drift little by little* into a state of mortal sin (reaching a point where you finally decide God just doesn't matter at all) than to get there by one sudden action, when up to that point you had tried hard to do what's right (although the latter is possible).

Those Nasty Words:
SIN and GUILT

The Catholic faith has often been accused of going overboard on emphasizing guilt for sins. The topic of "Catholic guilt" even comes up as a joke line in movies and on television. Whether or not that was true in the past, it's hardly the case today. Sometimes we're extremely uncomfortable even mentioning the phrase "committing sin." We replace it with softer phrases like "making poor decisions" and "failing to love as we should." Those phrases are accurate enough, but avoiding the word *sin* is not realistic.

There are two kinds of guilt. One is a heavy, depressing guilt that makes a person feel overall spiritually lousy and blinds him or her to his or her good qualities and even to the mercy of God. The other is normal, actually healthy guilt based on a realistic admission of one's wrong actions—sins. It's like the pain in the body that indicates something is wrong and needs healing. If a person ignores that pain or stifles it with painkillers, the problem causing the pain never gets attended to and healed.

The solution is balance: seeing both sides of us—the bright side and the dark side. Yes, we are wonderful in many, many ways. And, yes, we sin. Only when we recognize both sides can we make real progress in our relationship with God. As Jesus said, the truth will make us free.

Sometimes there's a difference between the action itself and the degree of guilt in the person committing it. For a person to be guilty, especially of a serious sin, three things have to be present:

1 the action has to be (seriously) wrong

2 the person must fully *know* this and choose to do it anyway

3 the person must be *free* to choose it or not choose it. This freedom can be limited from the outside, as when he or she is ordered to do something under threat of great harm or death; or from the inside, as when he or she suffers from a serious emotional disturbance.

It's also worth noting that it's easy to use #2 and #3 as escape holes—to claim that we didn't really know how wrong something was (when actually we did), or that we were helplessly overcome with strong feelings (when actually we *invited* and/or prolonged those feelings and did nothing to get rid of them).

56 conscience (39)

We often say, "Your conscience is what tells you when something you did, or are about to do, is wrong." Correctly understood, that's true, but it's also misleading because it sounds like conscience is *something other than you*. Not so. Conscience is a part of you; it's your ability to judge right from wrong.

We also often say, "You have to follow your conscience," and that's absolutely true. But again, conscience is not something separate from each of us that we're not responsible for. It's our moral compass, and we're responsible to see that it's set correctly; or, think of it as our moral muscle, and it's our responsibility to see that it's developed and works correctly.

Your conscience is what tells you when something you did, or are about to do, is wrong.

Can a person's conscience ever really screw up, such as truly thinking something wrong is actually right, or vice versa? Or can it ever not work at all?

Of course.

Children who are told over and over, from the time they are very young, that it's right and good to hate and even kill people of another race or religion are not going to have a correctly formed and functioning conscience, and that's not their fault.

Just like a muscle that's seldom or never used, conscience can function weakly or not at all from pure lack of use, as when a person decides, "Oh well…" about any temptation. For that, the person *is* responsible.

We are obligated to find out and consult the teaching of the Church in forming our conscience. Otherwise, we are deliberately setting out all on our own and ignoring the very people who have been trained and commissioned to teach and guide us. That's like being on a team but ignoring the manager and all the coaches.

57 the Ten Commandments *(39–40)*

Sometimes there's a moral situation that's hard to classify and clearly judge simply by reading the commandments. On the other hand, the Ten Commandments cover many more situations than it may appear in the simple, literal definition of their words. Each commandment below is followed by some further reflection on what it covers.

The commandments are sometimes presented principally as tests of obedience—if we're obedient enough to keep them, we'll get to heaven. But again, that makes heaven something we earn, which is not the case.

The commandments do indeed test our obedience sometimes, but that's not their principal purpose. God gave us the commandments in order to guide us to a good and happy life. They're the rules of a loving God who wants to see us happy and who doesn't want us hurting ourselves and one another.

1. You shall honor no other god than me.

Do not let anything become so important in your life that it leads you to disobey God. That's the same as worshiping a false god.

2. You shall not misuse the name of the Lord, your God.

Do not curse, which is using God's name to condemn someone. (That's more specific than using the crude language we commonly call cussing.) Do not use the name of God, Jesus, Christ, and other holy names simply as outlets of emotion, especially negative emotion.

3. Remember to keep holy the Sabbath.

Worship God at Mass on Sundays and holy days of obligation.

4. Honor your father and your mother.

Obey and respect all legitimate authority—within the family, the church, and civil societies such as the city, the state, etc.

5. You shall not kill.

Do not cause or allow unnecessary harm of any kind—physical, emotional, spiritual, or otherwise—to any person, including yourself. (This commandment covers *a lot* of moral territory!)

6. You shall not commit adultery.

Do not misuse your sexuality in any way. (This commandment likewise includes a lot of situations and actions.)

7. You shall not steal.

Do not take someone else's property or deface or damage it in any way. (This includes property that belongs to everyone, such as public buildings or street signs.)

8. You shall not bear false witness against your neighbor.

Do not lie, distort the truth, or withhold all or part of the truth (deliberately not tell it even though you are not directly asked) in dealing with anyone who has a right to know the truth. (A killer hired by organized crime does not have the right to know where the mayor is.)

9. You shall not covet your neighbor's wife.

Do not plan sexual activity that should not happen or expose yourself to influences such as pornography. (This is not the same as simply feeling normal sexual desires.)

10. You shall not covet your neighbor's goods.

Do not let yourself be so filled with jealousy, envy, or greed that you *would* take someone's money or property if you had the chance to get away with it.

58 the law of love *(40)*

Law and *love* may seem as though they don't belong together. "If you love someone, it should be because you really want to and feel like it, not because it's a law." But that ignores human nature and narrows love to a feeling. Love is more than that. We are called to love someone even when we don't want to be around him or her.

The *law of love* is contained in the *two great commandments*: "You shall love the Lord, your God with all your heart, with all your soul, and with all your mind," and "You shall love your neighbor as yourself" (Matthew 22:37, 39).

As Jesus himself said, all other laws come from these two. If you truly love someone, you will not damage his or her property, to use an obvious example.

We can be confused about the law of love if we think that love has to be full of (or at least frequently contain) romantic or warm feelings. Some love relationships do, as between husband and wife, parent and child, or good friends, and sometimes we feel a glow or even a thrill when we're praying to or worshiping God.

But at other times, obeying God—which is showing love for God—is difficult and does not produce warm, cozy feelings. We are called to love people we don't even like. Loving them means treating them justly, not doing or wishing them any harm, and coming to their assistance when they are in need.

> We are called to love people we don't even like.

By both his words and his example, Jesus expanded the law of love beyond basics. The law of love as Jesus taught and modeled it calls us to reach out in service to others beyond what is strictly required.

Loving Someone You REALLY Don't Like

Someone just said or did something that was monstrously unfair, stupid, uncalled for, awful, snobbish, mean, dreadful, and a whole bunch of similar adjectives. Maybe you were the victim, maybe some other totally wonderful, innocent person was, maybe both. Or perhaps the nasty deed happened some time ago, but you still remember it, and that person hasn't apologized. Or maybe someone is just plain constantly irritating...as you see it. *This is awful, and you don't deserve it!* (As you see it.) You'd like to *just smack*— but enough. You know the situation; you've been there.

How do you love that person or those persons in this situation? *You pray for him, her, or them.* Pray and mean it. Not a Please Change That Person! Prayer ("Dear God, please let ___ know how terribly he/she is acting and help him/her stop!"), but a prayer that asks for good things for that person or persons. God knows what they need.

Maybe they do need to change, and your prayer may help make the change happen. Whether that happens or not, what *will* happen, if you're sincere, is that your anger and resentment will diminish, and you'll be much more at peace. You may come to see that person differently. You may even begin to ask, "What was *my* part in this misunderstanding?"

59 the problem of evil *(40–41)*

Probably nothing causes people to doubt God more than the fact that horrendous injustice, tragedy, and suffering strike innocent people. Thousands of people die at the hands of terrorists. People ask why there is still so much sin and evil if Jesus has conquered it. Thousands of people die of cancer. People ask why God permits this when Jesus himself went about curing sick people.

The first type, the problem of *moral* evil, is more easily explained. God made human beings free to do good or to do evil. Strangely, without the freedom to do evil, good actions do not mean anything. If someone asked you on a terrific date *because he or she had no other choice,* it wouldn't exactly make you feel warm and chosen. Freedom is a 100% either/or package. There's no such thing as leaving human beings free to do,

> ...Without the freedom to do evil, good actions do not mean anything.

let's say, ten pounds of evil, but if they plan to do eleven pounds of it, God reaches down and stops them.

Jesus, who was God himself, was not untouchable by the forces of evil.

Physical evils, such as cancer and earthquakes are much more difficult for many people. Without book-length discussions, we can only say that God does not promise a perfect world. God *does* promise help to survive trials in this life and perfect happiness in the next life.

Some types of suffering and injustice exist not because individual people devise horrible acts, but because we as a people tolerate those conditions by not working hard enough to eliminate them. Some prime examples are hunger and poverty. This is sometimes called *social sin*.

Our faith calls us to trust in the goodness, faithfulness, and love of God who is able to draw good out of evil. The leading example of that is the death and rising of Jesus, God himself.

60 the world: run away or blend in? *(41–42)*

We Catholic Christians follow a crucified Savior who commanded us to love our enemies, forgive those who hurt us, and in general, to act as *he* would act. That makes us different—or it *should.* (If you were on trial for being a Christian, would there be enough evidence to convict you?) It also poses a question: How should we view and act toward the society we live in—which frequently does *not* operate on Christian values?

Even in early Christian times, some followers of Jesus had chosen one of two opposite attitudes, both of them wrong. The first was to consider the world essentially evil, dangerous, and something to be avoided as much as possible. (Today's version: Don't go to movies, don't go to dances, stay away from the mall, etc.) The second was to blend in with the world wherever need be or wherever convenient—or even wherever fun. (Today's version: You should follow Jesus, sure, but you have to be like other people, too, or you won't have a life.)

If you were on trial for being a **Christian,** would there be enough evidence to convict you?

That Good Old
Big Bad Peer Pressure

Peer pressure is not purely a middle-grades-through-college thing. (Even Nicodemus came to see Jesus secretly at night. Why? Fear of what *his middle-aged peers* would think!) But it's probably strongest during those years. Nearly all young people acknowledge peer pressure as a strong factor—in the lives of *other* young people. "I don't care what other people think" flows almost automatically from many young people who, at the same time, try very hard to wear the right clothes, fit in to the cool groups, say the approved things, and who smoke the joint they didn't really want or drink the beer they don't really like.

The "just say no" strategy has been urged so frequently that hearing it can be almost tiresome. It sounds like an unrealistically simple and supposedly easy solution invented by adults who don't live on the teen planet. Well, it *is* simple—but simple does not mean easy. No one ever said it was easy. Problem is, it's the only thing that works. It's based on the hard fact that you cannot control other people, but you can control yourself. We often don't realize how many young people make this simple-although-not-easy strategy work. Many people who grow up in drug cultures and gang-infested neighborhoods make it to their adult years while staying in charge of their own lives.

Catholics see that there is evil *in* the world and society, but this does not mean the world and society *are* evil and should be avoided. Quite the opposite: If we don't act in society to mend the evil in it, we let evil (temporarily) win. Jesus didn't gather his followers into a cave and advise them to stay there; he literally sent them out into the world. But he didn't say, "Blend in with everybody. Whatever they're doing, you can do, too. I've saved you, so what you do doesn't matter."

There are some things we simply cannot do, some lifestyles we simply cannot adopt, and still say we're following Jesus. There are times when a follower of Jesus has to look at what's going on around him or her and say, "That's *wrong*. I cannot be a part of it. I cannot even appear to go along with it. I will not be an, 'Oh, well, that's just how things are these days' pseudo-Christian."

61 the media *(42)*

Human beings have had media since the days of cave drawings and smoke signals. Media become more complex as time goes on, but they still serve their two basic purposes: to inform and to entertain.

A Christian viewer or listener needs to look for the attitude or message in a piece of information or entertainment when it deals with things that have a moral (right and wrong) dimension. It's easy to become passive about entertainment in particular, especially if it's cleverly produced and attractively packaged. Almost without realizing it, we can become influenced by what it says on issues such as honesty, the value of life, and the meaning of sexuality. "But it's just a show" and "But it was *funny*" are common excuses to go along with entertainment that is clearly contrary to what Jesus taught.

62 violence *(42–43)*

There's a difference between *force,* which occasionally is needed to stop an obviously unjust situation, and *violence,* which seeks to do harm just for the sake of doing so. Example: If an innocent person is being attacked, it will take some force to subdue the attacker, and that's legitimate. Doing more physical harm to the attacker than needed is violence, and that's *not* legitimate. The question in many situations is, "How do we subdue evil without engaging in that same evil and becoming evil ourselves?"

We live in a society that often glorifies might, violence, and retaliation for the slightest injury. When confronted with the temptation to use violence, especially when it seems (but only *seems*) justified, a Christian must ask the now familiar question, "What would Jesus do?"

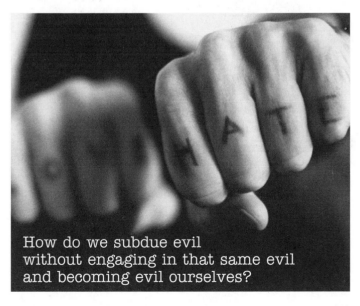

How do we subdue evil
without engaging in that same evil
and becoming evil ourselves?

63 honesty *(43)*

We live in a society where getting things is important. Often enough, they're good things, like enough money to live comfortably, good grades that will lead to a good job, and so forth. We're also conditioned to want them quickly and easily; sometimes we're even conditioned to feel we're *entitled* to them no matter what.

That makes honesty both in action and in speech (commandments seven and eight) a major issue. It goes beyond wanting physical items that belong to someone else, whether they're in the next locker or on a display shelf in a store. We face temptations in particular to take something we haven't earned, such as a

Being honest means being real.

paycheck we didn't fully work for or a good grade we didn't really study for.

It's tempting to see the goal as the only thing that matters (again, especially if it's something good in itself), and adopt a "whatever it takes" (to get what we want) perspective in reaching that goal. "Whatever it takes" becomes especially attractive when it's combined with, "But nobody's really getting hurt" and/or, "Everybody does it." But those are lies themselves. Somebody always gets hurt in some way or other, and it's not true that everybody is dishonest.

Being honest means being real. It means being the person God created us to be.

64 sexuality *(43–44)*

God created sexual actions to express and celebrate the love between a man and a woman who have promised themselves to one another until death and to give them the immense privilege of helping to create new human life.

Much of the world looks at that statement and says, "Narrow, limiting, and old-fashioned," or "Well, yeah, but let's get real." Actually, it's God who wants us to get real about our sexuality. When we fully realize what a spectacular gift our sexuality is, we begin to see the wisdom of God's "restrictions" on its use. It's like realizing that a diamond necklace is not meant to be used as a common door chain.

Recall what we said about the commandments in general. They're not just tests of obedience, and the sixth and ninth commandments about sexuality are not the narrow rules of an old-fashioned God who doesn't want to see us having too much fun. Like all the commandments, they're the rules of a loving parent who doesn't want us to hurt ourselves and one another.

The best proof of that is a list of all the negatives—all the pain, suffering, shattered lives, and canceled futures—that can happen when God's directions are not followed and sexuality is misused. The list is literally too long to make here, but it includes

For every person who may say or think, "I wish we had," there are thousands upon thousands who say or think, "I wish we hadn't."

things like abortion, date rape, sexually transmitted diseases, broken hearts, and children born into situations where they cannot be taken care of. The damage is physical, emotional, social, and spiritual.

Entertainment that presents sex as a carefree pleasure that everyone has a right to whenever they can get it—almost like an outing at an amusement park—almost never shows the damage. (That wouldn't be entertaining. *Real,* but not entertaining.)

God really does have a better idea. Following God's plan for sexuality in a world that regards that plan as unrealistic and silly is not easy, but it leads to the happiness God wants for us. The proof again is in the evidence of life itself and human experience: For every person who may say or think, "I wish we *had,*" there are thousands upon thousands who say or think, "I wish we *hadn't.*"

65 alcohol and drugs *(44)*

God commands us to care for our bodies and to use our minds to direct our actions correctly. It's wrong to intentionally do something that harms the body and/or puts our minds out of control to the point where we endanger others and ourselves.

Illegal, psychoactive substances always do both. For that reason, they are always wrong. It really is as simple as that. It makes no difference how many people say or act otherwise.

Illegal here includes *illegal for the user.* While some substances, like heroin, are illegal for anyone under any condition, others such as commonly prescribed painkillers are illegal for a user who is not taking them as prescribed by a doctor for a definite condition.

A mountain of inescapable evidence shows that, like many other sinful activities, the use of psychoactive drugs escalates.

Occasional experiments spiral into frequent and then addicted use with frightening speed. "It's only weed" turns into "It's just crystal meth," and the user comes to regard this drug-centered lifestyle as normal…merely misunderstood by nonusers.

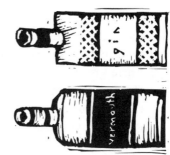

Unlike some Christian denominations, the Catholic Church does not teach that alcohol itself is evil. The Bible cites wine as a beverage of celebration, and the first public miracle of Jesus was changing water into wine at a wedding feast.

However, the Bible does strongly warn against an excess of alcohol. The mind- and mood-altering effects of alcohol often lead people to do things they would never intentionally do or even consider when sober. Evidence shows that, while alcohol is legitimate (that's *not* the same as *necessary*) when used reasonably, it's extremely dangerous and destructive when used to excess.

Few people—perhaps none—say, "I wish I had drunk more when I was younger." But literally millions say, "I wish I had never started drinking."

"It's my body and my life" is a lie. Someone who uses drugs or abuses alcohol always harms others, often severely. *ALWAYS*. The list of victims includes parents, whose every day is filled with worry; peers, who are recruited into alcohol or drug use; victims of rape (including date or acquaintance rape), robbery, vandalism, violence,

The mind- and mood-altering effects of alcohol often lead people to do things they would never intentionally do or even consider when sober.

and DUI; and spouses and children who are neglected. (No matter how much feeling an alcoholic or drug user may have for his or her children, he or she cannot be an effective parent. Period.)

There's nothing wrong with feeling good. But expecting to feel good all the time is unrealistic, and using chemical substances to get that feeling is wrong. There's also a huge difference between physical-emotional pleasure and genuine happiness. Legitimate pleasure can often be *part* of happiness, but it is not the same thing. The frequent use of chemicals to create the illusion of happiness actually makes true happiness—which God made for us—impossible.

P.S.

At some time or other, you have probably imagined living in a mansion. It may have been a massive stone structure a couple centuries old, full of high-ceilinged rooms with huge fireplaces, lit by candles in brackets on the walls, ornately carved wooden railings on winding staircases, and rounded towers at the corners. Or it may have been a state-of-the-art, modern architectural masterpiece, with an indoor pool, a sauna, a home movie theater, and rooms filled with the latest computer technology and gadgets for wireless living.

My favorite image of the Catholic Church is a mansion with *all* the above and more. We have so much cool old Catholic stuff

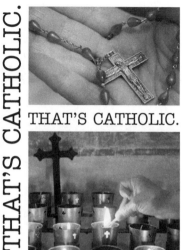

THAT'S CATHOLIC.

THAT'S CATHOLIC.

THAT'S CATHOLIC.

and so much cool new Catholic stuff! We have customs, traditions, and rituals that go back many centuries, and others that were designed expressly for today. We have huge cathedrals and cozy little chapels. We have ancient chant from hundreds of years ago and contemporary hymns that were written this year.

We have so many rooms in this Catholic mansion that you cannot spend a great deal of time in every one of them in one lifetime. So, you find the ones that speak to your heart and soul, and spend a lot of time being Catholic there.

You may choose to spend a good bit of time with very traditional prayers, such as the rosary. That's Catholic. You may feel called to give a great deal of time and energy to promoting causes such as Right to Life. That's Catholic. You may find yourself involved in working for social justice—fighting racism and poverty, for example—or building or rehabbing homes for people less fortunate. That's Catholic. Dipping your fingers into the holy water font and lighting a votive candle at a shrine in church, reading and studying the Book of Revelation to learn what some of the wildly colorful symbols mean, taking part in a respectful protest against unfair labor or housing practices... they're all ways of being Catholic.

It's a shame that some people visit only a couple rooms in our Catholic mansion, decide they're not interesting (or never take the time to really understand what's there), and eventually leave... or just hang out on the doorstep and go into the lobby once a year at Christmas.

It really is a cool old/new mansion. Spend some time getting to know it. I hope you decide, as the title of a book says,

I Like Being Catholic.

Other Related Liguori Publications Titles for Teens

HANDBOOK FOR TODAY'S CATHOLIC TEEN
ACTIVITY NOTEBOOK
ISBN 978-0-7648-1378-8

This activity notebook is a companion to *Handbook for Today's Catholic Teen*. It has pertinent, useful questions to connect subject matter with personal experience, draw conclusions, and formulate further questions. It also offers suggested activities to apply the content of the *Handbook* in practical ways.

UPS & DOWNS
Prayers By & 4 Teens
ISBN 978-0-7648-1881-3

A book of prayers written by teens for teens and focused on contemporary issues in their lives. Teens share their reflections and the words that help them cope with life's difficulties, rejoice in God's grace, and make the best decisions when faced with tough choices.

LIFE STRATEGIES FOR CATHOLIC TEENS
Tough Issues, Straight Talk
Jim Auer
ISBN 978-0-7648-1151-7

With an element missing from many teen books today, *Life Strategies for Catholic Teens* addresses the challenges young people face from a Catholic Christian perspective. In typical Jim Auer style, *Life Strategies for Catholic Teens* blends concrete examples, lively anecdotes, scriptural references, and appropriate quotations from sources that range from ancient proverbs to Shakespeare and popular song lyrics.

For prices and ordering information,
call us toll free at 800-325-9521
or visit our Web site, www.liguori.org.